WeightWatchers®

COOK!

150 brand new and delicious recipes to help you eat wisely

SIMON & SCHUSTER
A CBS COMPANY

Penny Stephens

First published in Great Britain by
Simon & Schuster UK Ltd, 2008
A CBS Company
Copyright © 2008, Weight Watchers International, Inc.
Simon & Schuster UK Ltd, Africa House,
64–78 Kingsway, London WC2B 6AH

3579108642

Weight Watchers, *POINTS* and **Core Plan** are trademarks of
Weight Watchers International, Inc., and are used under its control by
Weight Watchers (UK) Ltd.

Weight Watchers Publications Team
Jane Griffiths, Donna Watts, Nina McKerlie, Nina Bhogal and
Eileen Thornton
Photography by Steve Baxter
Styling by Rachel Jukes
Food preparation and styling by Carol Tennant
Design and typesetting by Jane Humphrey
Printed and bound in China

A CIP catalogue for this book is available from the British Library

Pictured on the front cover: Courgette and Pesto Pasta with Halloumi,
page 114
Pictured on the back cover: clockwise from left to right, Spanish Rice,
page 38; Steak and Onion Sandwich, page 30; Roasted Ragoût with
Borlotti Beans, page 118; Orange Profiteroles with Chocolate Sauce,
page 174
Pictured on the inside front flap: Twice Baked Herby Potatoes, page 152

POINTS® value logo: You'll find this easy to read *POINTS* value logo on every recipe throughout this book. The logo represents the number of *POINTS* values per serving each recipe contains. The easy to use *POINTS* **Plan** is designed to help you eat what you want, when you want – as long as you stay within your daily *POINTS* allowance – giving you the freedom to enjoy the food you love.

You'll find this distinctive **Core Plan**™ logo on every recipe that can be followed freely on the **Core Plan**. These recipes contain only foods that form part of the **Core Plan**.

Ⓨ This symbol denotes a vegetarian recipe and assumes that, where relevant, organic eggs, vegetarian cheese, vegetarian virtually fat free fromage frais and vegetarian low fat crème fraîche are used. Virtually fat free fromage frais and low fat crème fraîche may contain traces of gelatine so they are not always vegetarian. Please check the labels.

❄ This symbol denotes a dish that can be frozen.

Recipe notes
Egg size Medium, unless otherwise stated.
All fruits and vegetables Medium sized unless otherwise stated.
Raw eggs Only the freshest eggs should be used. Pregnant women, the elderly and children should avoid recipes with eggs which are not fully cooked or raw.
Recipe timings These are approximate and meant to be guidelines. Please note that the preparation time includes all the steps up to and following the main cooking time(s).
Polyunsaturated margarine Use brands such as Flora Light, St Ivel Gold, Benecol Light and Tesco Healthy Living Olive spread.
Rice If following the **Core Plan** remember to use brown rice. If using white rice, remember to calculate the *POINTS* values.
Core Plan If following the **Core Plan** you have a limited allowance of 2 teaspoons of healthy oil a day (olive, sunflower, safflower, flaxseed, rapeseed) to use in recipes as you choose.

contents

Whether you are following the *POINTS* **Plan** or the **Core Plan**, *Cook!*
is ideal. This fantastic new cookbook will help you plan your meals,
eat wisely and lose weight. It has been designed to work alongside
the Weight Watchers programme and it contains clear, easy to follow
recipes which will help you to create delicious and satisfying meals
for yourself, friends and family. All the recipes use fresh, healthy
ingredients, so you can eat delicious, vibrant, healthy foods and stay on
track with your weight loss.

There are 150 new recipes to choose from and some variations on
old favourites. So whether you are a confident cook or a novice in the
kitchen, you'll find plenty of variety and inspiration. There is something
for everyone in *Cook!* There are new lunch ideas, budget recipes, dishes
for the family, quick and easy recipes as well as great ways to impress
your guests. You'll also find a fantastic selection of sweet things to
tempt your taste buds, all with low *POINTS* values. There is also a
chapter on sauces and marinades which you can use to accompany
some of the recipes in this book or use with some of your own favourite
recipes.

In each chapter, you'll find recipes with the *POINTS* values clearly
shown, and half are suitable for the **Core Plan** (with the distinctive logo
by the title). A large proportion of the recipes are vegetarian and many
recipes suggest alternative ingredients to make a recipe vegetarian.
You'll also find suggestions throughout of recipes that work well
together – easily identifiable by the colourful 'Goes well with' boxes.

There is a **Core Plan** index providing the *POINTS* values of non core
foods in *POINTS* **Plan** recipes, so you know how much of your optional
weekly *POINTS* allowance you would use.

We hope you enjoy using *Cook!* and that it inspires you to eat wisely.

introduction

Feeling good about your food choices

Fruits of the Forest Steamed Pudding, page 170

Whether you are looking for a warming soup for lunch or dinner, or a fresh and delicious salad to share, you'll find a range of tempting choices here, all with low **POINTS** values. Try the Spiced Parsnip Soup with Parsnip Crisps or for something more filling, the Chilli and Bean Soup. For a light lunch, the Fresh Tuna Niçoise Salad is ideal. If you're having lunch with friends, try the Roasted Pumpkin and Pasta Salad. Perhaps something for your lunchbox – why not take an Avocado and Crab Salad or the Thai Style Chicken Salad to work?

soups and salads

Mussel broth with croûtes

Takes 20 minutes to prepare, 20 minutes to cook
9½ *POINTS* values per recipe
275 calories per serving

Serves 4 Ideal for summer eating.

1 kg (2 lb 4 oz) mussels (weight with shells)
850 ml (1½ pints) fish stock
1 garlic clove, sliced
2 shallots, sliced thinly
2 tomatoes, deseeded and diced
2 tablespoons freshly chopped tarragon

for the croûtes
1 garlic clove
8 × 15 g (½ oz) slices French baguette
low fat cooking spray

1 To clean the mussels, scrub off any dirt and remove any barnacles. Remove the beard, if any, that sticks out between the shells. Discard any that are already open or with a cracked shell.
2 In a large lidded saucepan, bring the stock to the boil. Add the garlic and shallots and simmer for 5 minutes. Add the mussels, cover and reduce the heat. Cook for 2–3 minutes until most of the shells have opened. Discard any that don't open.
3 Use a slotted spoon to remove the mussels. Remove the mussels from the shells of all but eight. Set aside the eight. Place the mussels and stock in a food processor and blend until smooth. Return to the pan with the tomatoes, tarragon and reserved mussels. Heat gently to warm through.
4 To make the croûtes, preheat the oven to Gas Mark 6/200°C/fan oven 180°C. Cut the garlic clove in half and rub the cut side over the bread. Spray with low fat cooking spray and place on a baking tray. Bake for 10–12 minutes until golden.
5 Serve the soup in warm bowls garnished with two mussels each and two croûtes on the side.

Cheesy broccoli soup

Ⓨ ❄ without the cheese

Takes 5 minutes to prepare, 15 minutes to cook
6 *POINTS* values per recipe
197 calories per serving

Serves 2 Broccoli not only has zero *POINTS* values but is packed with antioxidants and iron. It is especially delicious with cheese.

300 g (10½ oz) broccoli, stalks included
150 g (5½ oz) potato, diced
600 ml (1 pint) vegetable stock
1 teaspoon dried thyme
40 g (1½ oz) Stilton cheese, crumbled

1 Chop the broccoli florets and stalks into bite sized pieces and place in a large lidded pan with the potato, stock and thyme. Bring to the boil, cover and simmer for 15 minutes until the potato is tender.
2 Transfer to a liquidiser or use a hand held blender to blend the soup. Return to the pan to warm through, if necessary, and serve topped with the crumbled Stilton.

Tip Danish Blue is a great alternative to Stilton. It is quite salty though, so taste the soup first before seasoning it. The *POINTS* values will remain the same.

Goes well with: the Savoury Mini Muffins on **page 158**, for an extra 1 *POINTS* value per serving.

Creamy celery soup

ⓨ vegan ❄

Takes 10 minutes to prepare, 20 minutes to cook
0 *POINTS* values per recipe
56 calories per serving

Serves 2 Celeriac not only adds flavour to this zero *POINTS* value soup, it also thickens it and makes it creamy.

low fat cooking spray
1 onion, sliced
2 celery sticks, chopped, leaves reserved
200 g (7 oz) celeriac, peeled and diced
1 bay leaf
600 ml (1 pint) vegetable stock

1   Lightly coat a large lidded non stick pan with low fat cooking spray and heat until hot. Add the vegetables and stir fry for 3–4 minutes until beginning to soften.
2   Add the bay leaf and stock. Bring to the boil, cover and simmer for 20 minutes until the vegetables are soft. Remove from the heat, take out the bay leaf and blend until smooth, either with a hand held blender or transfer to a liquidiser.
3   Gently reheat the soup to warm it through. Serve garnished with the reserved celery leaves.

Tip Celeriac is a winter root vegetable with a hard texture like parsnip but with the flavour of celery. If you can't find it, use the equivalent weight in peeled and chopped potatoes, adding an extra celery stick, for a *POINTS* value of 1 per serving.

Spiced parsnip soup with parsnip crisps

ⓨ vegan ❄ **except the crisps**

Takes 30 minutes
5 *POINTS* values per recipe
92 calories per serving

Serves 4 Thick and warming, with homemade crisps on the side.

500 g (1 lb 2 oz) parsnips
low fat cooking spray
1 teaspoon ground cumin
1 teaspoon garam masala
1 litre (1¾ pints) vegetable stock
salt and freshly ground black pepper

1   Preheat the oven to Gas Mark 6/200°C/fan oven 180°C.
2   Peel all the parsnips, leaving one whole and cutting the rest into chunks. Lightly coat a large lidded pan with low fat cooking spray and heat until hot. Add the chopped parsnips and spices and stir fry for 1 minute. Add the stock, bring to the boil, cover and simmer for 10 minutes until the parsnips are tender. Remove from the heat and liquidise or blend with a hand held blender. Return the soup to the pan and warm through.
3   Meanwhile, using a vegetable peeler, cut the remaining parsnip into ribbons. Spread out on a baking tray and lightly coat with low fat cooking spray. Sprinkle over a little salt and freshly ground black pepper and bake for 5–10 minutes until golden and crisp.
4   Serve the soup hot with the parsnip crisps on the side.

Tips If you prefer a spicier soup, add ½ teaspoon chilli powder with the other spices.

You can make the soup in advance, but the crisps are best when fresh.

Creamy watercress and parsley soup

Takes 10 minutes
½ POINTS value per recipe
36 calories per serving

Serves 2 In this very quick soup, the sweetness of the parsley deliciously complements the pepperiness of the watercress.

400 ml (14 fl oz) vegetable stock
110 g (4 oz) watercress, chopped roughly, 2 sprigs reserved
15 g (½ oz) fresh parsley, chopped roughly
100 ml (3½ fl oz) skimmed milk
salt and freshly ground black pepper

1 In a large lidded saucepan, bring the stock to the boil. Add the chopped watercress, cover and simmer for 3 minutes.
2 Place the soup in a liquidiser or use a hand held blender to roughly blend. Add the parsley and blend again. The soup should be a vibrant green colour but still have pieces of leaf visible.
3 Return to the pan, add the milk, season and warm through. Serve garnished with the reserved watercress sprigs and lots of freshly ground black pepper.

Tip Try the same recipe using half rocket and half watercress. The **POINTS** values will remain the same.

Chilli and bean soup

vegan
Takes 25 minutes
6½ POINTS values per recipe
275 calories per serving

Serves 2 This hearty soup has a touch of chilli to make it warming.

low fat cooking spray
1 leek, sliced
250 g (9 oz) potatoes, peeled and diced
1 carrot, diced
1 celery stick, trimmed and chopped
2 garlic cloves, chopped
2 teaspoons chilli powder
1 x 410 g can kidney beans, drained
700 ml (1¼ pints) vegetable stock
2 tablespoons freshly chopped parsley, to garnish

1 Lightly coat a large lidded saucepan with low fat cooking spray and heat until hot. Add the leek and stir fry for 3 minutes. Add the potatoes, carrot, celery, garlic and chilli powder. Stir fry for a further 1 minute.
2 Add the beans and the stock. Bring to the boil, cover and simmer for 10 minutes until all the vegetables are tender.
3 Serve in warm bowls, garnished with the parsley.

Tip Any sort of canned bean will work in this soup – try butter beans, for a **POINTS** value of 2½ per serving.

Spicy beef and noodle soup

Takes 30 minutes
13 POINTS values per recipe
311 calories per serving

Serves 2 A tangy and slightly hot Oriental soup with strips of beef and noodles.

low fat cooking spray
300 g (10½ oz) lean rump beef, cut into thin strips
1 litre (1¾ pints) beef stock
2 lemon grass sticks, tough outer leaves removed, chopped
2 red chillies, deseeded and diced
juice 2 limes
125 g (4½ oz) thread egg noodles
75 g (2¾ oz) mange tout
110 g (4 oz) baby corn
coriander leaves, to garnish

1 Lightly coat a large lidded non stick pan with low fat cooking spray and heat until hot. Add the beef and stir fry for 3–5 minutes until browned all over.
2 Add the stock, lemon grass, chillies and lime juice. Bring to the boil, cover and simmer for 10 minutes until the beef is tender.
3 Add the noodles, mange tout and baby corn. Bring to the boil. Simmer gently for 5 minutes until the noodles are cooked and the vegetables tender. Garnish with coriander before serving.

Tip Try this recipe with the equivalent weight in skinless boneless chicken breast, for a **POINTS** value of 5½ per serving.

Winter slaw

Takes 10 minutes
2 *POINTS* values per recipe
93 calories per serving

Serves 1 Crunchy vegetables mixed into a creamy dressing make a delicious combination.

110 g (4 oz) white cabbage, sliced thinly
3 radishes, sliced thinly
50 g (1¾ oz) celeriac, peeled and grated
2 teaspoons wholegrain mustard
1 tablespoon low fat plain yogurt
1 teaspoon lemon zest
1 tablespoon pumpkin seeds
1 teaspoon sesame seeds
salt and freshly ground black pepper

1 Combine the vegetables in a bowl.
2 Mix together the mustard, yogurt and lemon zest, and season. Stir into the vegetables.
3 In a small non stick frying pan, dry fry the seeds until golden. This will only take a minute, so watch them carefully. Scatter over the slaw to serve.

Tips Try adding 1 teaspoon of hot horseradish to the dressing for an extra kick, for the same *POINTS* values.

75 g (2¾ oz) finely sliced fennel goes well in this salad, for no extra *POINTS* values.

Goes well with: the Herb Loaf on **page 32**, for an extra 3½ *POINTS* values per serving (2 slices each).

Spiced lentil dip with crudités

Ⓨ vegan

Takes 5 minutes to prepare + cooling time, 30 minutes to cook
4½ *POINTS* values per recipe
229 calories per serving

Serves 1 This makes a delicious alternative to houmous, which tends to be high in *POINTS* values.

50 g (1¾ oz) split red lentils
300 ml (10 fl oz) vegetable stock
½ teaspoon ground cumin
1 teaspoon curry powder
2 teaspoons sesame seeds

to serve
celery sticks
red pepper slices
carrot sticks
2 wholewheat Krisprolls

1 Place the lentils and stock in a small lidded saucepan. Bring to the boil and continue boiling for 10 minutes, then cover and cook for a further 20 minutes until the lentils are mushy. Keep an eye on the pan, as you may need to add extra water to the lentils if they get too dry. You should be able to mash the cooked mixture easily with a fork, to form a rough, slightly wet, purée – it will thicken on cooling.
2 Dry fry the spices and sesame seeds for 1 or 2 minutes until their aroma is released, then add to the lentil purée and stir well. Leave to cool before chilling.
3 Serve the dip with the vegetable sticks and slices as well as the Krisprolls.

Tip This is a great party dip or lunch box – you could also add strips of pitta bread (1 x 60 g/2 oz), in place of the Krisprolls, for a *POINTS* value of 5½ per serving.

Creamy mustard potato salad

Takes 15 minutes to prepare, 10–15 minutes to cook
3 *POINTS* values per recipe
342 calories per serving

Serves 1 This potato salad has a lovely, creamy mustard dressing and is especially good with beetroot and Quorn bacon.

150 g (5½ oz) new potatoes, scrubbed and halved if large
2 teaspoons wholegrain mustard
low fat cooking spray
2 Quorn bacon style rashers
1 tablespoon 0% fat Greek yogurt
3 cocktail beetroots, halved
a handful of rocket leaves, to serve

1   Bring a saucepan of water to the boil, add the potatoes and cook for 10–15 minutes until tender. Drain, and while still warm, mix with the mustard. Leave to cool.
2   Lightly coat a non stick frying pan with low fat cooking spray and cook the rashers for 2 minutes, turning once, until crispy. Set aside.
3   Mix the yogurt and beetroots into the potatoes. Chop the rashers into small pieces and sprinkle over the top. Serve with the rocket leaves.

Tip Keep the rocket leaves separate until you are ready to serve, otherwise they will wilt.

Roasted pumpkin and pasta salad

Y vegan

Takes 25 minutes to prepare, 40 minutes to cook
7½ *POINTS* values per recipe
219 calories per serving

Serves 4 Roasted vegetables give this colourful salad lots of lovely flavour, and the balsamic vinegar adds a delicious tang.

1 kg (2 lb 4 oz) pumpkin or butternut squash, peeled and cut into bite size pieces
2 carrots, cut into chunky batons
2 red onions, cut into wedges
1 orange pepper, cut into strips
16 cherry tomatoes, halved
2 rosemary sprigs
low fat cooking spray
150 g (5½ oz) small pasta shapes, e.g. fusilli
4 tablespoons balsamic vinegar
salt and freshly ground black pepper

1   Preheat the oven to Gas Mark 6/200°C/fan oven 180°C.
2   Place all the vegetables and the rosemary in a large roasting tray and spray with low fat cooking spray. Roast in the oven for 40 minutes until tender and beginning to char. You will need to turn them occasionally.
3   Meanwhile, bring a pan of water to the boil, add the pasta and cook according to the packet instructions. Drain and rinse in cold water.
4   Mix the vegetables into the pasta, season and drizzle over the balsamic vinegar. Allow to cool before serving.

Tip You could add four well cooked and chopped Quorn bacon style rashers, for a *POINTS* value of 2½ per serving.

Fresh tuna Niçoise salad

Takes 30 minutes
4 POINTS values per recipe
334 calories per serving

Serves 1 Fresh tuna is a great way to get your omega 3, plus it's quick to cook and very low in fat.

60 g (2 oz) new potatoes, halved if large
1 x 125 g (4½ oz) piece tuna
low fat cooking spray
25 g (1 oz) fine green beans, trimmed
1 Little Gem lettuce, leaves separated
½ x 400 g can artichokes in water, drained
1 egg, hard boiled, peeled and quartered
1 tablespoon natural virtually fat free fromage frais
½ teaspoon lemon zest
salt and freshly ground black pepper

1   Bring a pan of water to the boil, add the potatoes and cook for 10–15 minutes until tender.
2   Meanwhile, heat a griddle pan or non stick frying pan until hot. Spray the tuna with low fat cooking spray and cook for 5–8 minutes (depending on thickness), turning once, until just cooked through. Remove and set aside.
3   Spray the beans with low fat cooking spray and cook in the pan used for the tuna, turning occasionally, for 2–3 minutes until tender. Remove from the heat and allow to cool.
4   When the potatoes are ready, drain, refresh in cold water, and drain again. Arrange on a plate with the beans, lettuce and artichokes. Top with the tuna and egg quarters.
5   Mix together the fromage frais, lemon zest and 1 teaspoon water. Season and then drizzle over the salad.

Tips If making as a lunch, keep the dressing in a separate pot until ready to eat, otherwise the salad will wilt.

You could serve this as a warm salad – just keep the potatoes, tuna and green beans warm and then simply serve mixed together with the other ingredients.

Chicken rice salad

Takes 10 minutes to prepare, 20–25 minutes to cook
4 *POINTS* values per recipe
311 calories per serving

Serves 1 Brown rice has a great nutty flavour and is more filling than white. Cook it in stock to add extra flavour. White balsamic makes the salad look nicer since it doesn't stain the food.

300 ml (10 fl oz) chicken or vegetable stock
50 g (1¾ oz) brown rice
75 g (2¾ oz) cooked, skinless boneless chicken breast, sliced
8 red grapes, halved
1 spring onion, sliced
1 teaspoon orange zest
2 teaspoons white balsamic (or ordinary balsamic) vinegar

1 In a lidded saucepan, bring the stock to the boil and add the rice. Cover and cook for 20–25 minutes until tender. Drain any excess stock and leave to cool.
2 Stir in the chicken, grapes and spring onion.
3 Mix together the orange zest and balsamic vinegar and then stir into the rice salad and serve.

Tips You can make this salad the night before and let the flavours mingle.

Spice it up with 1 teaspoon of freshly chopped red chilli. The *POINTS* values will remain the same.

Avocado and crab salad

Takes 10 minutes
10½ *POINTS* values per recipe
214 calories per serving

Serves 2 The lime and chilli give this salad a delicious Thai flavour.

1 x 170 g can crab meat, drained
½ large mango, peeled and chopped
½ teaspoon finely diced red chilli
zest and juice 1 lime
a good handful of chopped Iceberg lettuce leaves
1 small avocado, peeled and sliced
8 cherry tomatoes
salt and freshly ground black pepper

1 Mix together the crab, mango, chilli and lime zest and half the juice. Season.
2 Divide the lettuce between two plates and spoon the crab mixture on top. Serve with the avocado slices, cherry tomatoes and the remaining lime juice drizzled over.

Tip Try this mixture with a 200 g can of drained tuna in brine or water instead of the crab meat. The *POINTS* values will remain the same.

Thai style chicken salad

❄ chicken only

Takes 1 hour

18½ POINTS values per recipe

227 calories per serving

Serves 4 Marinating the chicken gives it extra flavour and salting the cucumber draws out the liquid making it deliciously crunchy.

4 x 75 g (2¾ oz) skinless boneless chicken thighs

1 tablespoon fish sauce

2 teaspoons finely diced red chilli

1 lemon grass stick, sliced

1 garlic clove, crushed

2 tablespoons lemon juice

2 teaspoons artificial sweetener

1 cucumber

110 g (4 oz) flat rice noodles

salt

mixed leaves, to serve

1 Preheat the oven to Gas Mark 6/200°C/fan oven 180°C.

2 Place the chicken in a lidded non metallic, ovenproof dish. Mix together the fish sauce, chilli, lemon grass, garlic, lemon juice and sweetener and pour over the chicken. Cover and leave at room temperature for 20 minutes.

3 Meanwhile, cut the cucumber into ribbons using a vegetable peeler. Sprinkle with salt and set aside for 10 minutes.

4 Roast the chicken, uncovered, in its dish for 30 minutes until golden and cooked through. Set aside to cool slightly, then cut into slices.

5 Bring a large pan of water to the boil and cook the noodles according to the packet instructions. Drain and keep warm.

6 Rinse the cucumber in cold water and pat dry with kitchen paper. Toss into the noodles with the mixed leaves and serve with the chicken.

Tip Serve this salad warm or cold for lunch. If cooling and chilling for lunch, keep the leaves separate, otherwise they will wilt.

Whenever you are short of time you need a selection of quick and tasty recipes that you can prepare in no time at all – such as the Steak and Onion Sandwich, the Cheesy Fusilli Bake or the Spanish Rice. All are guaranteed to satisfy. The Florentine Pizza is ideal for lunch or tea and the Pea and Ham Frittata couldn't be easier. The recipes here use everyday ingredients and many are ready in under 30 minutes.

quick and easy

Butternut squash and goat's cheese penne

Takes 25 minutes
4 POINTS values per recipe
315 calories per serving

Serves 1 The sweetness of the butternut squash complements the tangy goat's cheese and sage.

50 g (1¾ oz) dried penne pasta
low fat cooking spray
150 g (5½ oz) butternut squash, peeled, deseeded and chopped into bite size pieces
1 garlic clove, sliced
3 sage leaves, shredded
salt and freshly ground black pepper
25 g (1 oz) soft goat's cheese, crumbled or cut into small pieces, to serve

1 Bring a pan of water to the boil, add the pasta and cook according to the packet instructions. Drain, reserving 2 tablespoons of cooking liquid, and set aside.

2 Lightly coat a medium non stick frying pan with low fat cooking spray and heat until hot. Add the butternut squash and stir fry for 5 minutes or until tender. Add the garlic and sage and cook for a further minute.

3 Add the pasta and reserved cooking liquid, and stir through until hot. Remove from the heat, season and serve with the goat's cheese on top.

Tip If you don't like goat's cheese, use 25 g (1 oz) reduced fat Cheddar cheese, grated over the top. The *POINTS* values will remain the same.

Florentine pizza

Takes 30 minutes
12½ *POINTS* values per recipe
383 calories per serving

Serves 2 Placing the pizza dough in the oven for a short while helps it to rise more quickly, and reduces the preparation time.

1 x 145 g packet pizza dough
300 g (10½ oz) spinach
1 garlic clove, crushed
2 tablespoons sun dried tomato purée
2 eggs
salt and freshly ground black pepper

1 Preheat the oven to Gas Mark 7/220°C/fan oven 200°C.

2 Make up the dough according to the packet instructions, dividing it to make two pizzas. Roll out to circles of approximately 20 cm (8 inch) diameter and place on a baking tray (you may need two). Put in the oven for 2 minutes so that it begins to rise.

3 Cook the spinach in a steamer, or in a pan with 3 tablespoons water, for 3–4 minutes until wilted. Drain well and, when cool enough to handle, squeeze out any excess water and chop roughly. Mix with the garlic and season.

4 Spread the tomato purée over the pizza bases and top with the spinach, making a well in the middle. Bake for 5 minutes, then remove from the oven. Crack an egg into the middle of each pizza, so that it is contained within the spinach, and bake for a further 8–10 minutes until the bases are crispy.

Tip Eat hot or cool it and then pack to enjoy for lunch.

quick and easy

Warm cheesy tomato salad

Takes 15 minutes
4½ *POINTS* values per recipe
285 calories per serving

Serves 1 Plum tomatoes are oval shaped and have lots of flavour. If you can't find them, use tomatoes on the vine instead.

1 tablespoon pine nuts
2 plum tomatoes, halved
15 g (½ oz) mature Cheddar cheese, grated finely
a handful of mixed salad leaves
1 tablespoon balsamic vinegar
1 medium slice granary bread, toasted

1 Preheat the grill to medium.
2 Place the pine nuts in a small non stick frying pan and dry fry over a medium heat for 1 or 2 minutes until golden.
3 Place the tomatoes on a baking tray, cut side up. Sprinkle with the cheese and grill for 5–6 minutes until beginning to brown.
4 Put the salad leaves on a plate and place the tomatoes on top. Sprinkle over with the pine nuts and drizzle with the balsamic vinegar. Serve with the toast on the side.

Steak and onion sandwich

Takes 15 minutes
4½ *POINTS* values per recipe
294 calories per serving

Serves 1 Piling hot meat on to bread is always a favourite and this minute steak with balsamic fried onions is delicious.

1 x 80 g (3 oz) lean minute or frying steak
low fat cooking spray
½ small red onion, sliced thinly
1 tablespoon balsamic vinegar
2 medium slices granary bread
salt and freshly ground black pepper
a handful of rocket leaves, to serve

1 Trim any excess fat from the steak and season on both sides. Lightly coat a small non stick frying pan with low fat cooking spray and heat until hot. Add the steak and cook, turning once, for 2–3 minutes until beginning to brown. Remove from the pan and keep warm.
2 Spray the pan again with low fat cooking spray and, when hot, add the onion. Cook over a medium heat for 5 minutes until soft and browned. Stir in the balsamic vinegar and remove from the heat.
3 Place the steak on one of the slices of bread and top with the onion and pan juices, followed by the rocket and the other slice of bread.

Tip If you prefer, use a 110 g (4 oz) piece of French baguette instead, for a *POINTS* value of 6½ per serving.

quick and easy

Chick pea tabbouleh

Takes 15 minutes
6 *POINTS* values per recipe
181 calories per serving

Serves 2 This is an easy way to make couscous very tasty without adding lots of ingredients.

1 x 110 g packet coriander and lemon couscous
200 ml (7 fl oz) boiling water
4 cm (1½ inch) piece cucumber, peeled and diced
25 g (1 oz) sultanas
½ x 410 g can chick peas, drained
3 tablespoons chopped mixed herbs, e.g. parsley, thyme, tarragon

1 Place the couscous in a large bowl and pour over the boiling water. Cover and leave to soak for 10 minutes.
2 Fluff the couscous with a fork and add the remaining ingredients. Toss to mix before serving.

Tip This makes a great lunch for work too, and can be prepared the night before and chilled.

Herb loaf

Takes 15 minutes to prepare, 30 minutes to cook + cooling
21½ *POINTS* values per recipe
211 calories per serving

Serves 6 (2 slices each) This is based on the French 'Cake aux Herbes' and is enjoyed as a lunch dish or handed around in small pieces with drinks.

low fat cooking spray
150 g (5½ oz) low fat polyunsaturated margarine, melted and cooled slightly
2 eggs, separated
150 g (5½ oz) self raising flour
2 garlic cloves, crushed
25 g (1 oz) green and black olives, chopped
1½ tablespoons capers in brine, rinsed
5 tablespoons freshly chopped mixed herbs, e.g. parsley, chives, sage, tarragon, thyme, dill, basil
2 egg whites

1 Preheat the oven to Gas Mark 4/180°C/fan oven 160°C. Lightly coat a 900 g (2 lb) loaf tin with low fat cooking spray.
2 Pour the melted margarine into a large bowl and beat in the 2 egg yolks. Add the flour and beat in with the garlic, olives, capers and herbs.
3 Whisk all the egg whites until they hold stiff peaks and then gradually fold into the other mixture.
4 Spoon into the prepared tin and bake for 30 minutes until golden and set – a skewer inserted in the centre should come out clean. Cool for 10 minutes in the tin before turning out.
5 Serve warm or cold.

Tip Store in an airtight container in the fridge for up to 3 days.

Serving suggestion Serve with a zero *POINTS* value green salad.

Cheesy fusilli bake

Takes 15 minutes
11½ *POINTS* values per recipe
294 calories per serving

Serves 2 This is a really quick pasta bake. Try using fresh pasta which, although more expensive, has a better flavour and cooks in only 4 minutes.

150 g (5½ oz) fresh fusilli pasta
50 g (1¾ oz) mange tout, cut into strips
1 x 400 g can whole cherry tomatoes
1 x 125 g packet reduced fat mozzarella, drained and sliced
salt and freshly ground black pepper
a handful of basil leaves, to garnish

1 Bring a large pan of water to the boil, add the pasta and cook according to the packet instructions. Add the mange tout for the final minute of cooking time. Drain well and return both the pasta and the mange tout to the pan.
2 Add the tomatoes to the pasta, put back on the heat and cook for 1–2 minutes until hot. Season.
3 Preheat the grill to medium. Spoon the pasta mixture into an ovenproof dish. Top with the mozzarella and grill for 2–3 minutes until the cheese is bubbling. Serve scattered with the basil leaves.

Tip If you can't find tinned cherry tomatoes, use a can of chopped tomatoes with added herbs for extra flavour.

Halloumi pitta

Takes 10 minutes
5½ *POINTS* values per recipe
340 calories per serving

Serves 1 Pepperdew peppers are small, fairly hot peppers which come in jars with a piquant dressing. They have zero *POINTS* value so are great to keep in the fridge.

70 g (2½ oz) halloumi light, sliced
1 wholemeal pitta bread
a handful of mixed leaves

for the salsa
1 pepperdew pepper, cut into thin strips, plus 2 teaspoons juice from jar
2 cm (¾ inch) piece cucumber, diced
1 teaspoon finely chopped red onion
1 tablespoon finely chopped coriander leaves

1 To make the salsa, place the pepperdew pepper in a small bowl. Combine with the juice from the jar, the cucumber, onion and coriander.
2 Preheat the grill to medium and grill the halloumi slices for 3–4 minutes, until golden. At the same time, grill the pitta bread for 1 minute until warm.
3 Slit open the pitta bread and fill with the halloumi, salad leaves and salsa.

Tip Make a pot of this salsa to keep in the fridge for up to 3 days, only adding the coriander when required – it's great with grilled meats and fish or to jazz up a salad.

quick and easy

BLT muffin

Takes 10 minutes
6 *POINTS* values per recipe
264 calories per serving

Serves 1 A quick fix breakfast, lunch or tea. This classic combo piled into a muffin is both satisfying and low in *POINTS* values.

2 rashers lean back bacon
1 English muffin, split
1 Cos lettuce leaf, torn
1 small tomato, sliced
1 tablespoon Weight Watchers mayonnaise dressing

1 Preheat the grill to medium and cook the bacon, turning occasionally, for up to 5 minutes, until cooked to your liking.
2 Toast both halves of the muffin until golden.
3 Place the lettuce on one toasted half, followed by the tomato slices and the bacon. Drizzle with the mayonnaise dressing, then place the other muffin half on top.

Ⓨ **Tip** For a vegetarian version, use two Quorn bacon style rashers instead of the lean back bacon, for a *POINTS* value of 4 per serving.

Parma ham bruschetta

Takes 20 minutes
9½ *POINTS* values per recipe
242 calories per serving

Serves 2 These tasty rounds of French bread, baked with a topping of fresh tomatoes, garlic, capers and Parma ham, are ideal as a starter or as a quick lunch.

1 small baguette (125 g/4½ oz), sliced diagonally into
   6 rounds
low fat cooking spray
3 large tomatoes on the vine, chopped
1 tablespoon capers, chopped roughly
1 garlic clove, crushed
6 slices Parma ham
12 basil leaves, to garnish

1 Preheat the oven to Gas Mark 6/200°C/fan oven 180°C. Place the bread slices on a baking tray and spray with low fat cooking spray.
2 Mix together the tomatoes, capers and garlic and pile on to the bread. Top each with a slice of Parma ham and bake for 10–12 minutes until the bread is golden and crisp.
3 Serve three rounds each, garnished with the basil leaves.

Tips Try this recipe with three rashers of cooked and chopped lean back bacon instead of the Parma ham, for a *POINTS* value of 5 per serving.

Ⓨ For a vegetarian option, omit the Parma ham and top each toast with 2 teaspoons low fat soft cheese before baking, for a *POINTS* value of 3½ per serving.

quick and easy

Spicy lamb stir fry

Takes 15 minutes
11½ POINTS values per recipe
380 calories per serving

Serves 2 Make this quick stir fry as spicy as you like by adding more or less chilli.

150 g (5½ oz) lean lamb leg steaks, cut into thin strips
1 x 300 g bag of fresh stir fry vegetables
1 red chilli, deseeded and diced
3 tablespoons light soy sauce
2 x 150 g packet Amoy straight to wok medium noodles

1 Heat a wok or large non stick frying pan until hot. Add the lamb and dry fry until browned all over.
2 Add the vegetables, chilli and 3 tablespoons water. Stir fry for 3–4 minutes until the vegetables are just tender.
3 Add the soy sauce and noodles and heat through. Serve immediately in warm bowls.

Tip Try this recipe with 110 g (4 oz) raw tiger prawns instead of the lamb, for a **POINTS** value of 4½ per serving.

Spanish rice

Takes 30 minutes
21½ POINTS values per recipe
368 calories per serving

Serves 4 Deliciously satisfying.

250 g (9 oz) dried brown rice
1 x 400 g can chopped tomatoes with herbs
200 g (7 oz) cooked, skinless boneless chicken breast, sliced
1 x 230 g packet of mixed seafood – prawns, mussels, squid
150 g (5½ oz) frozen peas
2 teaspoons smoked paprika (optional)

1 Bring a pan of water to the boil and cook the rice according to the packet instructions. Drain well.
2 Place all the ingredients, including the rice, in a large lidded non stick frying pan and heat gently.
3 Add 1 tablespoon water, cover and simmer for 10 minutes until piping hot.
4 Serve in large bowls.

Tip Smoked paprika, or pimenton, adds a smoky flavour and is available in most larger supermarkets in the herbs and spice section.

Mackerel with Parma ham

Takes 25 minutes to prepare, 15 minutes to cook
17 *POINTS* values per recipe
540 calories per serving

Serves 2 The horseradish mash adds a touch of warmth to this very flavourful dish.

350 g (12 oz) potatoes, chopped
1 tablespoon horseradish sauce
4 slices Parma ham, cut in half lengthways
4 x 60 g (2 oz) mackerel fillets, cut in half lengthways

1 Bring a large pan of water to the boil, add the potatoes and cook for 15 minutes until tender. Drain, reserving 2 tablespoons of the cooking liquid.
2 Mash the potatoes with the reserved cooking liquid and the horseradish. Keep warm.
3 Preheat the grill to medium. Wrap a strip of Parma ham around each mackerel fillet and grill, skin side up, for 8–10 minutes, turning occasionally, until browned and cooked through.
4 Serve the mackerel wrapped in Parma ham with the mash on the side.

Serving suggestion Serve with steamed broccoli, for no additional ***POINTS*** values.

quick and easy

Papparadelle with creamy peppered steak

Takes 30 minutes
25 *POINTS* values per recipe
411 calories per serving

Serves 4 Papparadelle is a wide form of tagliatelle and it's ideal for creamy sauces since it has plenty of surface area to cling to.

1 x 25 g packet dried porcini mushrooms
200 ml (7 fl oz) boiling water, to cover
300 g (10½ oz) dried papparadelle pasta
low fat cooking spray
2 red onions, sliced thinly
300 g (10½ oz) stir fry steak strips
110 g (4 oz) low fat soft cheese
freshly ground black pepper

1 Place the mushrooms in a bowl and pour over sufficient boiling water to just cover. Set aside to soak.

2 Meanwhile, bring a large pan of water to the boil, add the pasta and cook according to the packet instructions. Drain and keep warm.

3 Lightly coat a non stick frying pan with low fat cooking spray and heat until hot. Add the onions and stir fry for 5 minutes until brown and soft.

4 Season the steak strips with freshly ground black pepper and add to the pan. Stir fry for 2–3 minutes until cooked through.

5 Tip the mushrooms and the soaking liquid into the pan. Let it sizzle and then add the soft cheese. Stir in to make a creamy sauce.

6 Toss the creamy beef mixture into the papparadelle and serve.

Tip Dried porcini mushrooms make a great store cupboard standby. They have an intense mushroom flavour and with a *POINTS* value of 0, they make an excellent addition to risottos and stews.

quick and easy

Smoked haddock pots

Takes 15 minutes to prepare, 30 minutes to cook
9 *POINTS* values per recipe
188 calories per serving

Serves 4 For a great lunch dish, serve with two wholewheat crispbreads and a zero *POINTS* value side salad, for an additional *POINTS* value of 2 per serving.

150 g (5½ oz) spinach
a kettle full of boiling water
low fat cooking spray
2 tomatoes, sliced
350 g (12 oz) smoked haddock, skinned and cut into pieces
4 eggs, beaten
2 teaspoons Dijon mustard
6 tablespoons skimmed milk
freshly ground black pepper

1   Preheat the oven to Gas Mark 4/180°C/fan oven 160°C. Place the spinach in a colander and wash well, then pour over the boiling water until it wilts. Drain and, when cool enough to handle, squeeze out any excess water with your hands. Chop roughly.
2   Lightly coat 4 x 200 ml (7 fl oz) ovenproof ramekins with low fat cooking spray. Divide the spinach between the pots, then place a couple of slices of tomato on top of the spinach, followed by equal amounts of the haddock.
3   Mix together the eggs, mustard and milk. Pour over the fish and sprinkle with freshly ground black pepper – the haddock is quite salty so you shouldn't need any salt. Place on a baking tray and bake for 30 minutes until set.
4   Serve in the pots.

Tip Try using 75 g (2¾ oz) smoked salmon per person instead of the haddock, for a *POINTS* value of 3 per serving.

Mackerel pâté

Takes 5 minutes
10 *POINTS* values per recipe
201 calories per serving

Serves 2 This quick and easy spread is great served on wholewheat crispbread with a little watercress on the side.

75 g (2¾ oz) smoked mackerel, skinned
40 g (1½ oz) low fat soft cheese
2 tablespoons 0% fat Greek yogurt
2 teaspoons finely chopped fresh dill
salt and freshly ground black pepper

to serve
4 wholewheat crispbreads
snipped chives
a few sprigs of watercress

1   Flake the mackerel into a small bowl.
2   Add the soft cheese, yogurt and dill. Mix well. Taste and then season.
3   Serve on top of the crispbreads, garnished with chives and accompanied by sprigs of watercress.

Tips Try adding a ½ teaspoon lemon zest for extra flavour.

If you can't find dill, try 1 tablespoon chopped parsley. 1 small, chopped spring onion works well too. The *POINTS* values will remain the same.

Pea and ham frittata

Takes 25 minutes
7½ *POINTS* values per recipe
300 calories per serving

Serves 2 A frittata is a substantial omelette made with lots of vegetables. It's also ideal for using up left-overs in the fridge.

60 g (2 oz) frozen peas
150 ml (5 fl oz) boiling water, to pour over
low fat cooking spray
200 g (7 oz) potatoes, cut into 2 cm (¾ inch) cubes
2 onions, sliced thinly
3 eggs, beaten
60 g (2 oz) wafer thin smoked ham, chopped

1 Place the peas in a bowl and pour over boiling water. Leave to defrost.
2 Lightly coat a non stick frying pan with low fat cooking spray and heat until hot. Add the potatoes and fry until beginning to brown. Add the onions, spray with low fat cooking spray and cook, stirring occasionally, for 5 minutes until lightly caramelised.
3 Drain the peas, stir in to the eggs and add to the pan. Scatter over the ham. Leave to cook for 2–3 minutes until just set.
4 Preheat the grill to medium and brown the frittata under the grill for 2–3 minutes until golden. Serve hot.

Tips If you want to use left over cooked vegetables, stir in carrots, broccoli or leeks with the eggs in step 3. The *POINTS* values will remain the same.

Try using the equivalent weight in smoked salmon instead of the ham. The *POINTS* values will remain the same.

quick and easy

At the end of a long week, there's nothing more satisfying then a delicious curry on a Friday night. Try the Beef Rhogan Josh or the Creamy Aubergine Curry with Bombay Potatoes. All are equally delicious and low in **POINTS** values, so you could even have them every night of the week if you wish.

For those cold evenings, why not try a rich and warming casserole? Both the Boston Baked Beans and Irish Stew are delicious and take no time at all to prepare. Just put them in the oven and let them cook. With this fabulous range of low **POINTS** value recipes to choose from, you'll be spoilt for choice.

curries and
casseroles

Tofu with green Thai curry sauce

Ⓥ vegan
Takes 15 minutes to prepare, 20 minutes to cook
12 *POINTS* values per recipe
325 calories per serving

Serves 2 Cooking tofu gently in the curry sauce allows it to absorb all the delicious flavours.

2 tablespoons green Thai curry paste
125 g (4½ oz) tofu, cubed
½ x 400 ml reduced fat coconut milk
200 ml (7 fl oz) vegetable stock
200 g (7 oz) sweet potato, peeled and cubed
75 g (2¾ oz) sugar snap peas
1 small red pepper, deseeded and sliced
a handful of sliced spring onion, to garnish

1 Preheat a lidded saucepan until hot. Put the paste and the tofu in the saucepan and stir fry for 1–2 minutes.
2 Add the coconut milk, stock and sweet potato. Bring to the boil, cover and simmer for 15 minutes until the potato is just tender.
3 Add the sugar snap peas and pepper. Cook for a further 5 minutes.
4 Serve garnished with sliced spring onion.

Tip For an extra treat, serve with coconut rice. For 2 people, cook 110 g (4 oz) Thai or long grain rice until tender, then drain. Meanwhile, dry fry 1 tablespoon desiccated coconut and toss into the rice before serving. This will be an additional *POINTS* value of 4 per serving.

Spiced lamb pittas

Takes 15 minutes to prepare + 20 minutes marinating,
  15 minutes to cook
15 *POINTS* values per recipe
382 calories per serving

Serves 2 These lamb skewers are cooked on the barbecue or under the grill, stuffed into warm pittas and then drizzled with minted yogurt.

350 g (12 oz) lean leg of lamb, cubed
2 teaspoons tandoori curry powder
3 tablespoons 0% fat Greek yogurt
1 garlic clove, crushed
1 onion, cut into wedges

to serve
2 pitta breads
10 mint leaves, shredded
2 cm (¾ inch) piece cucumber, peeled and diced
2 tablespoons 0% fat Greek yogurt

1 Place the lamb in a non metallic bowl. Mix together the tandoori powder, yogurt and garlic and pour over the lamb. Stir well and set aside to marinate at room temperature for 20 minutes.
2 Preheat the grill to medium. Thread the lamb and onion on to skewers, brushing over any excess yogurt mixture. Grill for 12–15 minutes until beginning to char.
3 To serve, warm the pitta breads under the grill. Mix together the mint, cucumber and yogurt. Split the pittas. Remove the meat and onions from the skewers, stuffing them into the pittas. Serve with the yogurt mixture.

Tip Instead of lamb, use the equivalent weight of skinless boneless chicken breast, cut into chunks, for a *POINTS* value of 6 per serving.

7½ POINTS VALUE

Creamy aubergine curry

 vegan ❄

Takes 25 minutes to prepare, 20 minutes to cook

10½ *POINTS* values per recipe

147 calories per serving

Serves 4 A creamy yet spicy curry. You can temper the heat by reducing the number of chillies.

for the paste

2 red chillies, deseeded and chopped roughly

2 garlic cloves, chopped

2 tablespoons freshly chopped coriander leaves

½ teaspoon ground coriander

½ teaspoon ground cumin

2 lime leaves, shredded

½ small onion, chopped roughly

2 cm (¾ inch) piece fresh root ginger, chopped

for the curry

2 aubergines, weighing approx 450 g (1 lb), cut lengthways into thin slices

low fat cooking spray

4 tomatoes on the vine, halved

1 x 400 ml can reduced fat coconut milk

1 Place all the ingredients for the paste in a food processor and blend until smooth. You may need to add 1 or 2 tablespoons of water.

2 Heat a griddle pan or non stick frying pan until hot. Spray the aubergine slices with low fat cooking spray and cook for 1–2 minutes until beginning to char. You may have to do this in batches.

3 Lightly coat a deep frying pan with low fat cooking spray and heat until hot. Add the paste and stir fry for 1 minute. Add the tomatoes and cook for 2 minutes before adding the aubergine and coconut milk. Simmer for 20 minutes before serving.

Tip You can make double the quantity of paste and freeze to use again.

Goes well with: the Spiced Lentil Dip with Crudités on **page 16** as a side dish or starter, for an extra 4½ *POINTS* values per serving.

Saag paneer

Ⓥ

Takes 30 minutes

7 *POINTS* values per recipe

155 calories per serving

Serves 2 Paneer is an Indian cheese available from larger supermarkets or specialist stores. Serve this dish as an accompaniment or on its own.

225 g (8 oz) spinach, chopped roughly

a kettle full of boiling water

low fat cooking spray

110 g (4 oz) paneer, cubed

1 red chilli, deseeded and chopped (optional)

2 garlic cloves, chopped

2 cm (¾ inch) piece fresh root ginger, peeled and grated

2 teaspoons garam masala

2 tablespoons whipping cream

salt and freshly ground black pepper

coriander leaves, to serve

1 Place the spinach in a large colander and pour over boiling water until it has just wilted. Set aside to drain.

2 Lightly coat a non stick frying pan with low fat cooking spray and heat until hot. Add the paneer and fry for 3–4 minutes until the cubes are golden. Add the chilli, if using, garlic, ginger and garam masala. Stir fry for 1–2 minutes.

3 Remove the pan from the heat. Stir in the spinach and 4 tablespoons water. Return to the heat and simmer for 10 minutes, then stir in the cream. Season and garnish with coriander leaves, before serving.

Beef red curry

Takes 20 minutes

21½ *POINTS* values per recipe

289 calories per serving

Serves 4 Red Thai curry paste tends to be hotter than the green, so be careful how much you use.

low fat cooking spray

300 g (10½ oz) lean rump steak, cut into pieces

2 tablespoons red Thai curry paste

1 green pepper, sliced

150 g (5½ oz) baby corn

½ x 400 ml can reduced fat coconut milk

300 ml (10 fl oz) vegetable stock

110 g (4 oz) beansprouts

2 x 150 g packet straight to wok Udon noodles

a handful of freshly chopped coriander, to garnish

1 Heat a large lidded saucepan until hot. Spray with low fat cooking spray and add the steak. Stir fry for 2–3 minutes until brown.

2 Add the paste, pepper and baby corn. Cook for a further 2–3 minutes until beginning to brown.

3 Add the coconut milk and stock. Bring to the boil, cover and simmer for 10 minutes until the beef is tender.

4 Add the beansprouts and noodles. Cook for 1–2 minutes until hot, then serve in warm bowls garnished with the coriander.

Tip Prawns work well with red Thai curry paste too. Replace the beef with prawns, adding 150 g (5½ oz) cooked, peeled prawns at the same time as the beansprouts, for a *POINTS* value of 4½ per serving.

Winter hotpot
with herby cobbler

Takes 30 minutes to prepare, 1 hour 20 minutes to
cook
13½ *POINTS* values per recipe
273 calories per serving

Serves 4 A great winter warmer, with a lovely,
doughy cobbler on the top.

for the casserole
low fat cooking spray
2 onions, cut into wedges
200 g (7 oz) potatoes, peeled and cut into chunks
150 g (5½ oz) sweet potato, peeled and cut into
chunks
250 g (9 oz) baby turnips, trimmed and halved
300 g (10½ oz) baby carrots, trimmed
1 fennel bulb, sliced
500 ml (18 fl oz) vegetable stock
1 bay leaf
1 tablespoon cornflour

for the cobbler
125 g (4½ oz) wholemeal self raising flour (reserve
2 teaspoons)
25 g (1 oz) low fat polyunsaturated margarine
2 teaspoons dried mixed herbs
4 tablespoons skimmed milk
salt and freshly ground black pepper
freshly chopped parsley, to garnish

1 Preheat the oven to Gas Mark 4/180°C/fan oven
160°C.
2 Lightly coat a large lidded ovenproof casserole
dish with low fat cooking spray and heat until hot.
Add the onions and stir fry for 5 minutes until
beginning to brown. Add the remaining vegetables,
stock and bay leaf. Bring to the boil. Cover and
transfer to the oven to cook for 1 hour.

3 To make the cobbler, place the flour in a bowl,
add the margarine and rub in using your fingertips
until the mixture resembles breadcrumbs. Stir
in the herbs and season lightly. Add the milk and
bring together to form a ball.
4 Dust the work surface with the reserved flour
and divide the dough into eight equal pieces. Roll
each into a ball, then flatten slightly.
5 Blend the cornflour with 2 tablespoons water.
Remove the casserole from the oven, take off the
lid and stir in the cornflour paste, mixing well.
Place the cobblers on top of the vegetables. Return
to the oven, uncovered, for 15–20 minutes until the
cobbler is risen and golden. Serve garnished with
freshly chopped parsley.

Tip Fennel adds a slightly aniseed flavour. If you
prefer, you can swap it for two sticks of chopped
celery. The *POINTS* values will remain the same.

Sausage and lentil casserole

Takes 30 minutes to prepare, 30 minutes to cook
24 *POINTS* values per recipe
341 calories per serving

Serves 4 Rich and warming, this is real comfort food.

low fat cooking spray
8 low fat sausages (400 g/14 oz total weight)
4 shallots, halved if large
2 garlic cloves, sliced
150 ml (5 fl oz) red wine
110 g (4 oz) Puy lentils
400 ml (14 fl oz) beef stock
2 teaspoons dried mixed herbs
450 g (1 lb) potatoes, peeled and chopped
salt and freshly ground black pepper

1 Lightly coat a large lidded pan with low fat cooking spray and heat until sizzling. Add the sausages and cook for 4–5 minutes until browned all over. Add the shallots and stir fry for 3–4 minutes, then add the garlic and cook for a further minute.
2 Add the wine and let it bubble for a minute before adding the lentils, stock and herbs. Bring to the boil, cover and simmer for 30 minutes until the lentils are soft and the sausages cooked through.
3 Meanwhile, boil the potatoes in plenty of water for 20 minutes until soft.
4 Drain the potatoes, reserving a little of the cooking liquid, and mash with the reserved liquid. Season and serve with the casserole.

Serving suggestion Serve with steamed cabbage, for no additional *POINTS* values.

Ⓨ Tip For a vegetarian version, use 8 vegetarian sausages and substitute vegetable stock for the beef stock, for a *POINTS* value of 5 per serving.

Pumpkin stew

Ⓨ

Takes 40 minutes
13 *POINTS* values per recipe
232 calories per serving

Serves 4 It's best to make this wonderfully colourful stew in the autumn when there are plenty of different pumpkins to choose from. If you prefer it not to be spicy, omit the chilli.

250 g (9 oz) potatoes, cut into chunks
300 g (10½ oz) pumpkin, peeled, deseeded and cut into chunks
low fat cooking spray
1 red onion, cut into wedges
2 garlic cloves, chopped
1 red chilli, deseeded and diced (optional)
1 red pepper, deseeded and sliced
1 x 198 g can sweetcorn, drained
1 x 400 g can butter beans, drained
1 x 410 g can chopped tomatoes
1 vegetable stock cube, crumbled
75 g (2¾ oz) feta cheese, crumbled

1 Bring a large pan of water to the boil, add the potatoes and pumpkin and parboil for 10 minutes. Drain and set aside.
2 Lightly coat a large non stick saucepan with low fat cooking spray and heat until hot. Add the onion and stir fry for 5 minutes. Add the garlic, chilli, if using, and pepper. Cook for a further minute.
3 Add the potatoes, pumpkin, sweetcorn, butter beans, tomatoes and stock cube. Stir to mix, adding 125 ml (4 fl oz) water. Simmer gently for 10 minutes until the vegetables are tender. Serve sprinkled with the feta cheese.

Tip If pumpkin is not in season, you can use butternut squash instead.

Chunky Thai vegetable curry

Ⓥ vegan
Takes 30 minutes
3 *POINTS* values per recipe
117 calories per serving

Serves 4 This uses an oil free red curry paste which can be made in advance and kept in the fridge for up to 5 days.

for the paste
1 teaspoon ground coriander
1 small red onion, chopped
1 lemon grass stick, chopped
2 garlic cloves, crushed
1 bird's eye chilli, deseeded and chopped roughly
2 cm (¾ inch) piece fresh root ginger, peeled and chopped

for the curry
low fat cooking spray
250 g (9 oz) sweet potato, peeled and cut into chunks
150 g (5½ oz) broccoli florets
150 g (5½ oz) cauliflower florets
1 red pepper, deseeded and sliced
150 g (5½ oz) baby corn
250 ml (9 fl oz) vegetable stock

1 To make the paste, place all the ingredients in a food processor and blend until it forms a coarse paste.
2 Lightly coat a large non stick frying pan with low fat cooking spray and heat until hot.
3 Add the paste and stir fry for 1 minute. Add all the vegetables and cook, stirring, for 2–3 minutes.
4 Add the stock, reduce the heat and simmer for 10 minutes until the vegetables are just tender. You may need to add extra water if the mixture gets too dry.

Beef rhogan josh

Takes 25 minutes to prepare, 1 hour to cook
5½ *POINTS* values per recipe
266 calories per serving

Serves 2 This medium spiced curry thickens up beautifully while cooking. Don't be put off by the length of cooking time – you can actually walk away and let it cook on its own.

low fat cooking spray
200 g (7 oz) lean steak, cubed
1 onion, sliced
1 green pepper, sliced
4 cm (1½ inch) piece fresh root ginger, peeled and grated
2 garlic cloves, crushed
1 teaspoon crushed chilli flakes
4 cardamom pods, seeds only
2 teaspoons ground cumin
2 teaspoons turmeric
2 teaspoons ground coriander
3 tablespoons low fat plain yogurt
1 x 400 g can chopped tomatoes

1 Lightly coat a large lidded pan with low fat cooking spray and heat until hot. Add the meat and cook for 3–4 minutes until browned all over. Remove from the pan and set aside.
2 Spray the pan again, add the onion and pepper and stir fry for 5 minutes until beginning to brown.
3 Add the ginger, garlic and spices. Cook for a further minute before adding the yogurt, the tomatoes and finally the meat.
4 Stir in 300 ml (10 fl oz) water, bring to the boil, cover and reduce the heat. Leave to simmer for 1 hour until the meat is tender.

Tip Serve with 150 g (5½ oz) cooked brown rice per serving, for an additional ***POINTS*** value of 3 per serving.

Prawn pilaff

Takes 15 minutes to prepare, 35 minutes to cook

16½ *POINTS* values per recipe

300 calories per serving

Serves 4 A pilaff is a spiced rice dish which usually has meat or vegetables, but this version uses prawns.

low fat cooking spray

2 onions, sliced thinly

2 green chillies, deseeded and diced

1 teaspoon garam masala

1 teaspoon turmeric

juice 1 lemon

225 g (8 oz) brown rice

1 litre (1¾ pints) vegetable stock

225 g (8 oz) prawns, cooked and peeled

110 g (4 oz) frozen peas

4 tablespoons freshly chopped coriander, to garnish

1 Lightly coat a lidded non stick frying pan with low fat cooking spray and heat until hot.

2 Add the onions and stir fry for 5 minutes until soft.

3 Add the chilli, spices, lemon juice and rice. Cook, stirring, for 1 minute.

4 Add the stock and bring to the boil. Cover and cook for 30 minutes until the rice is tender and most of the stock has been absorbed.

5 Stir in the prawns and peas and cook for a further 5 minutes until hot. Serve garnished with coriander.

Bombay potatoes

Ⓥ vegan

Takes 10 minutes to prepare, 15 minutes to cook

5 *POINTS* values per recipe

80 calories per serving

Serves 4 These spicy potatoes make a great accompaniment to any curry and a nice change from rice.

450 g (1 lb) new potatoes, halved if large

low fat cooking spray

2 teaspoons Bombay spice

1 teaspoon black onion seeds (optional)

75 ml (3 fl oz) hot vegetable stock

1 Bring a lidded pan of water to the boil, add the potatoes and cook for 15 minutes until tender. Drain well.

2 Lightly coat a small saucepan with low fat cooking spray and heat until hot. Add the Bombay spice and black onion seeds, if using. Cook for 1 minute until sizzling.

3 Add the potatoes and hot stock. Cook for 1–2 minutes until most of the stock has evaporated.

Tips Try adding 300 g (10½ oz) steamed cauliflower florets to this recipe. Simply add them to the saucepan with the spices for no extra *POINTS* values.

Bombay spice is a combination of various spices, including coriander seeds, cumin and turmeric and can be found in the herbs and spices section of the supermarket.

Goes well with: the Beef Rhogan Josh on **page 60**, for an extra 3 *POINTS* values per serving.

Boston baked beans

**Takes 15 minutes to prepare + overnight soaking time,
3½ hours to cook**
19½ POINTS values per recipe
240 calories per serving

Serves 4 Long, slow cooking allows the beans to absorb all the wonderful flavours in this delicious recipe. Start the process the night before by leaving the beans to soak in a large pot of cold water.

250 g (9 oz) dried haricot beans, soaked in water
  overnight
150 g (5½ oz) smoked lean back bacon, chopped
2 teaspoons artificial sweetener
1 tablespoon wholegrain mustard
2 tablespoons Worcestershire sauce
8 small shallots, peeled and halved if large
4 garlic cloves

1 Drain the beans, which have been soaked overnight, and place in a large lidded ovenproof and flameproof casserole. Add enough water to just cover the beans, bring to the boil and continue boiling for 10 minutes. Reduce the heat, cover and simmer for 1 hour until just tender.
2 Preheat the oven to Gas Mark 2/150°C/fan oven 130°C.
3 Add the remaining ingredients to the casserole, cover and place in the oven for 2 hours. Remove the lid and cook for a further 30 minutes to thicken the sauce.

Ⓥ Tip For a vegetarian version, omit the bacon and add 2 teaspoons smoked paprika so that you retain that lovely smoky flavour, for a **POINTS** value of 2½ per serving.

Irish stew

Takes 10 minutes to prepare, 2 hours to cook
18½ *POINTS* values per recipe
400 calories per serving

Serves 4 The classic combination of lamb and potatoes works well in this chunky and flavoursome stew.

4 x 110 g (4 oz) lamb chops, trimmed of excess fat
600 g (1 lb 5 oz) potatoes, quartered
2 large onions, quartered
2 large carrots, peeled and cut into chunks
40 g (1½ oz) red split lentils
700 ml (1¼ pints) vegetable stock
salt and freshly ground black pepper

1 Preheat the oven to Gas Mark 1/140°C/fan oven 120°C.
2 Place all the ingredients in a large lidded ovenproof casserole. Cover and cook in the oven for 1½ hours, then remove the lid and continue cooking for a further 30 minutes to thicken the stew. Season before serving.

Serving suggestion Serve with steamed green beans, for no additional *POINTS* values.

Goes well with: the Brussels Sprouts and Parsley Purée on **page 154**, for an extra ½ *POINTS* value per serving.

Beef and butter bean stew

Takes 20 minutes to prepare, 1 hour 50 minutes to cook
15 *POINTS* values per recipe
237 calories per serving

Serves 4 This is a wonderfully hearty beef stew. Adding butter beans lends a lovely creamy texture to the gravy.

low fat cooking spray
450 g (1 lb) lean casserole beef, cubed
2 onions, chopped
2 garlic cloves, crushed
1 leek, chopped
600 ml (1 pint) beef stock
2 carrots, peeled and chopped
1 x 410 g can butter beans, drained
4 teaspoons horseradish, to serve

1 Lightly coat a large lidded saucepan with low fat cooking spray and heat until hot. Add the beef and stir fry until browned all over.
2 Add the onions and continue cooking for 3 minutes before adding the garlic and leek. Cook for a further 2 minutes.
3 Add the stock and carrots and bring to the boil. Cover and simmer for 1½ hours until the meat is tender.
4 Add the butter beans and continue to cook, uncovered, for a further 20 minutes.
5 Serve with a teaspoon of horseradish per bowl.

Tip Try borlotti beans in this stew instead of the butter beans, for a *POINTS* value of 4 per serving.

Chicken tagine with lemon couscous

❄ stew only

Takes 30 minutes to prepare + 10 minutes soaking, 20 minutes to cook

12½ POINTS values per recipe

413 calories per serving

Serves 2 The word tagine actually refers to the earthenware dish, with a funnel shaped top, in which the food is cooked. This dish comes from North Africa and is usually a vegetable or meat recipe cooked with cinnamon and other spices.

low fat cooking spray

2 x 125 g (4½ oz) skinless boneless chicken breasts

1 red pepper, deseeded and sliced

1 onion, chopped

2 garlic cloves, crushed

1 teaspoon ground cinnamon

1 teaspoon ground cumin

½ teaspoon turmeric

2 tomatoes, chopped

250 ml (9 fl oz) chicken stock

1 x 411 g can apricots in natural juice, drained and sliced

for the couscous

125 g (4½ oz) couscous

150 ml (5 fl oz) hot chicken stock

75 g (2¾ oz) steamed green beans, chopped into 5 cm (2 inch) pieces

zest and juice ½ lemon

salt and freshly ground black pepper

2 tablespoons freshly chopped coriander, to garnish

1 Spray a lidded non stick frying pan with low fat cooking spray and heat until hot. Add the chicken breasts whole and cook for 3 minutes, turning once, until browned on both sides. Remove from the pan.

2 Spray the pan again and add the pepper and onion. Stir fry for 5 minutes until just tender. Add the garlic and spices and continue cooking for 1 minute. Return the chicken to the pan with the tomatoes and stock. Cover and simmer over a low heat for 15 minutes. Add the apricots and cook for another 5 minutes until the chicken is tender.

3 Meanwhile, to prepare the couscous, place it in a bowl, pour over the hot stock and cover with cling film. Set aside to soak for 10 minutes. Fluff with a fork and then stir in the beans, lemon zest and juice. Season.

4 Serve the chicken tagine with a pile of the couscous and the coriander sprinkled over.

Tip If you like spicy food, add 1 teaspoon of hot chilli powder with the spices in step 2, for no additional **POINTS** values .

Preparing meals for the whole family can often be difficult if everyone wants something different. But in this chapter you'll find a range of recipes that are sure to satisfy. The Spring Vegetable Lasagne and Veggie Shepherd's Pie are always family favourites. Or you could try Chicken Fricassée, Lamb and Mint Burgers or Chicken Teriyaki – all quick to prepare and certain to keep all the family happy. There's truly something for everyone.

food for the

family

Turkey kebabs

Takes 25 minutes to prepare, 15–20 minutes to cook
12 *POINTS* values per recipe
353 calories per serving

Serves 2 These kebabs are quick and easy to make and the lightly spiced peanut sauce adds an Indonesian touch.

175 g (6 oz) turkey breast fillet, sliced into strips
100 g (3½ oz) sweet potato, peeled and cut into
    chunks
½ red onion, cut into wedges
½ red pepper, deseeded and cut into slices
low fat cooking spray
2 x 60 g (2 oz) pitta bread
1 tablespoon wholenut peanut butter
¼ teaspoon chilli powder (optional)

1 Preheat the grill to medium. Thread the turkey strips, sweet potato, onion and pepper alternately on to four short skewers. Spray with low fat cooking spray and grill for 15–20 minutes, turning occasionally, until the meat and vegetables are cooked through.
2 Warm the pitta breads under the grill for 1–2 minutes.
3 Meanwhile, place the peanut butter in a small pan with the chilli powder, if using, and 3 tablespoons water. Place on a low heat and stir until well combined and of a pouring consistency. If the mixture gets too thick, add a little more water.
4 Remove the turkey and vegetables from the skewers. Slit open the pitta breads and fill with the turkey and vegetables. Drizzle over the peanut sauce and serve.

Serving suggestion If you prefer, serve the kebabs with rice (cook 60 g/2 oz dried rice per person) instead of the pitta bread, for a *POINTS* value of 7 per serving.

Tip You may wish to use reduced fat smooth peanut butter, for a *POINTS* value of 5 per serving.

Fish crumble

❄

Takes 20 minutes to prepare, 40 minutes to cook
17 *POINTS* values per recipe
278 calories per serving

Serves 4 Baked beans add a touch of sweetness and their tomato sauce goes well with the fish and peas. Make double the topping and freeze for later.

300 g (10½ oz) smoked haddock fillet, skinned and
    chopped into bite size pieces
100 ml (3½ fl oz) skimmed milk
1 x 415 g can reduced sugar and salt baked beans
75 g (2¾ oz) frozen peas

for the crumble topping
50 g (1¾ oz) wholemeal flour
40 g (1½ oz) low fat polyunsaturated margarine
50 g (1¾ oz) oats
2 teaspoons dried mixed herbs
salt and freshly ground black pepper

1 Preheat the oven to Gas Mark 5/190°C/fan oven 170°C. Place the fish in the bottom of an ovenproof dish.
2 Put the milk, beans and peas in a saucepan and heat for 3–4 minutes until the peas have defrosted and the mixture is hot. Pour over the fish.
3 To make the crumble topping, place the flour in a large bowl, add the margarine and rub it in using your fingertips until it resembles breadcrumbs. Stir in the oats and herbs with a little seasoning.
4 Sprinkle over the fish and bake for 40 minutes until golden and hot.

Serving suggestion Serve with steamed broccoli, for no additional *POINTS* values.

Spring vegetable lasagne

Takes 35 minutes to prepare, 40 minutes to cook
16½ *POINTS* values per recipe
303 calories per serving

Serves 4 Lasagne is always a family favourite. If you make it with vegetables and a light but creamy sauce, it is a surprisingly low fat and healthy meal.

low fat cooking spray
6 spring onions, sliced
175 g (6 oz) carrots, peeled and diced
1 fennel bulb, sliced
110 g (4 oz) baby corn, halved
1 x 500 g jar passata
2 garlic cloves, crushed
½ vegetable stock cube, crumbled
6–9 lasagne sheets (total weight 140 g/5 oz), fresh or no precook variety
8 cherry tomatoes, halved
40 g (1½ oz) mature Cheddar cheese, grated
salt and freshly ground black pepper

for the sauce
25 g (1 oz) low fat polyunsaturated margarine
25 g (1 oz) plain flour
450 ml (16 fl oz) skimmed milk

1 Lightly coat a large non stick saucepan with low fat cooking spray and heat until hot. Add the spring onions, carrots, fennel and baby corn. Stir fry for 3 minutes. Add the passata, garlic and stock cube. Reduce the heat and simmer for 10 minutes until the vegetables are tender. Season.
2 Preheat the oven to Gas Mark 5/190°C/fan oven 170°C.
3 To make the sauce, melt the margarine in a pan, add the flour and mix well. Cook for 1 minute, then remove from the heat. Gradually add the milk, beating well after each addition to make a smooth paste before adding more. Return to the heat and cook gently, stirring continuously, until the sauce thickens, just coating the back of a spoon. Season.
4 Place a third of the vegetable mixture on the base of an ovenproof lasagne dish. Spoon over 2 tablespoons of the sauce and top with 2 or 3 (depending on size) pasta sheets. Spoon half the remaining vegetable mixture on top of the pasta, top with half the remaining sauce and another 2 or 3 pasta sheets. Repeat with the remaining vegetable mixture and pasta. Spoon over the remaining sauce.
5 Scatter over the tomatoes, sprinkle with the cheese and bake for 40 minutes until golden and bubbling.

Serving suggestion Serve with a zero *POINTS* value green salad.

Tip You can try other vegetables in the lasagne – broccoli or courgettes work well. The *POINTS* values will remain the same.

Sesame beef noodles

Takes 25 minutes
11½ POINTS values per recipe
266 calories per serving

Serves 2 A quick and easy stir fry packed with vegetables and sprinkled with sesame seeds, which are a good source of calcium.

low fat cooking spray
200 g (7 oz) lean rump steak, cut into thin strips
75 g (2¾ oz) green beans, trimmed and halved
2 heads pak choi, leaves divided
8 cherry tomatoes
3 tablespoons light soy sauce
125 g (4½ oz) thread egg noodles
2 teaspoons sesame seeds

1 Spray a large non stick frying pan with low fat cooking spray. When hot, add the steak and beans and stir fry for 3–4 minutes until beginning to brown. Add the pak choi and tomatoes and stir fry for 2 minutes before adding the soy sauce and cooking for a further 1 minute.
2 Meanwhile, bring a pan of water to the boil, add the noodles and cook according to the packet instructions. Drain.
3 In a small non stick frying pan, dry fry the sesame seeds for 1–2 minutes until golden and beginning to pop.
4 Serve the stir fry on top of the noodles, sprinkled with the sesame seeds.

Tip Chicken also works well in this recipe – cut the same weight of skinless boneless chicken breast into thin strips and stir fry as above, for a **POINTS** value of 5 per serving.

Pork kiev

Takes 10 minutes to prepare, 40 minutes to cook
8½ POINTS values per recipe
251 calories per serving

Serves 2 Pork fillet is a good lean cut that cooks quickly and easily. Here it is stuffed with garlic and herbs.

2 tablespoons freshly chopped parsley
2 garlic cloves, chopped
1 teaspoon olive oil
250 g (9 oz) pork fillet
3 tablespoons fresh brown breadcrumbs
1 egg white, lightly beaten
salt and freshly ground black pepper
2 tablespoons unsweetened apple sauce, to serve

1 Preheat the oven to Gas Mark 4/180°C/fan oven 160°C.
2 Mix together the parsley, garlic and oil with 2 teaspoons water. Make a long slit in the pork fillet and stuff with the herb mixture.
3 Season the breadcrumbs and place in a shallow bowl. Dip the pork fillet in the egg white and then coat in the breadcrumbs.
4 Place on a baking tray. Cook for 40 minutes until golden and cooked through. Slice the fillet and serve with the apple sauce.

Tip This recipe works well with chicken too – allow a 150 g (5½ oz) skinless boneless chicken breast per person, for a **POINTS** value of 3½ per serving.

Serving suggestion Serve with cooked carrots and broccoli, for no extra **POINTS** values.

food for the family

Lamb and mint burgers

❄ burgers only

Takes 30 minutes

22½ *POINTS* values per recipe

280 calories per serving

Serves 4 Home made burgers are not only delicious but, with lean meat, they are also low in fat.

for the burgers
low fat cooking spray
1 onion, diced finely
1 garlic clove, crushed
500 g (1 lb 2 oz) lean lamb mince
2 tablespoons freshly chopped fresh mint
salt and freshly ground black pepper

for the mint relish
2 spring onions, sliced thinly
4 cm (1½ inch) piece cucumber, diced
2 tablespoons freshly chopped mint
1 apple, cored and diced
2 teaspoons lemon juice

to serve
a few tomato slices
a few Iceberg lettuce leaves

1 Lightly coat a frying pan with low fat cooking spray and heat until hot. Add the onion and garlic and cook gently for 7–10 minutes until soft. Remove from the heat.

2 In a bowl, mix together the lamb, mint, cooked garlic and onion. Season well. Form the mixture into four burgers.

3 Spray the pan again with low fat cooking spray and heat until hot. Add the burgers and cook for 5–8 minutes on both sides until golden (or to your liking).

4 Meanwhile, to make the mint relish, combine all the ingredients in a bowl and set aside until required.

5 To serve, wrap the burgers in the Iceberg lettuce leaves, top with a tomato slice and a spoonful of mint relish.

Tips Try these burgers with 500 g (1 lb 2 oz) minced pork, adding the zest of 1 orange to the meat instead of the mint, for a *POINTS* value of 4½ per serving.

For the mint relish, try using the juice of a small orange instead of lemon juice, for no extra *POINTS* values.

Goes well with: the Tangy Chilli Relish on **page 199**, for no extra *POINTS* values.

Lemon and artichoke risotto

Takes 40 minutes
8 *POINTS* values per recipe
325 calories per serving

Serves 2 Canned artichokes in water are a great zero *POINTS* value store cupboard standby. Combine them with peas and rice for a lovely, fresh tasting risotto.

low fat cooking spray
4 spring onions, sliced
2 garlic cloves, sliced
125 g (4½ oz) brown rice
600 ml (1 pint) vegetable stock
zest and juice 1 small lemon
50 g (1¾ oz) frozen peas
1 x 400 g can artichokes in water, drained
50 g (1¾ oz) low fat soft cheese
2 tablespoons chopped coriander

1 Lightly coat a large non stick frying pan with low fat cooking spray and heat until hot. Add the spring onions and garlic and stir fry for 2 minutes until the onions have softened.
2 Add the rice and cook for 1 minute before adding the stock, a little at a time. Ensure the stock is virtually all absorbed before adding any more. Continue until all the stock is used and the rice tender.
3 Stir in the lemon zest and juice, the peas, artichokes and soft cheese. Warm through to defrost the peas and serve garnished with the coriander.

Smoked ham pasta with olives and lemon

Takes 20 minutes
18 *POINTS* values per recipe
335 calories per serving

Serves 4 This makes a tasty yet simple midweek supper and is delicious with a green salad and cucumber.

300 g (10½ oz) tagliatelle pasta
75 g (2¾ oz) mange tout
16 cherry tomatoes on the vine, halved
150 g (5½ oz) wafer thin smoked ham, cut into strips
60 g (2 oz) stoned black olives in brine, drained and halved
zest and juice 1 lemon
salt and freshly ground black pepper
lemon wedges, to serve

1 Bring a large pan of water to the boil, add the pasta and cook according to the packet instructions. Add the mange tout for the last minute of cooking time. Drain, reserving 4 tablespoons of the cooking liquid and return the pasta, mange tout and reserved liquid to the pan.
2 Add the remaining ingredients and mix well. Leave on a low heat for 1–2 minutes until everything is hot. Season and serve immediately with lemon wedges to squeeze over.

Tips Using the zest and juice of a lime also works well in this dish. Also, a generous handful of rocket or watercress makes a good addition - just toss it in at the last minute, for no additional *POINTS* values.

You can replace the ham with 125 g (4½ oz) smoked salmon trimmings for a change. The *POINTS* values will be the same.

Chicken teriyaki

Takes 20 minutes to prepare + 10 minutes marinating
18 *POINTS* values per recipe
348 calories per serving

Serves 4 Teriyaki sauce gives a lovely sweet and
sour tang and you don't have to marinate for long
for the flavours to be absorbed into the chicken.

450 g (1 lb) skinless boneless chicken breast, cut into
   strips
3 tablespoons teriyaki sauce
low fat cooking spray
6 spring onions, sliced
110 g (4 oz) baby corn
200 g (7 oz) green beans, halved
200 g (7 oz) beansprouts
3 x 150 g packets Amoy straight to wok medium
   noodles

1 Place the chicken strips in a non metallic bowl,
pour over the teriyaki sauce and leave to marinate
for 10 minutes.
2 Lightly coat a large non stick frying pan or
wok with low fat cooking spray and heat until hot.
Remove the chicken from the dish using a slotted
spoon and add to the pan, reserving any left
over sauce, and stir fry for 3–4 minutes until the
chicken is beginning to brown.
3 Add the spring onions, baby corn and beans. Stir
fry for 2–3 minutes.
4 Add the beansprouts and noodles, plus the
reserved marinade, and continue cooking for
1–2 minutes until everything is hot. If the mixture
gets too dry, add 1–2 tablespoons water. Serve
immediately.

Chicken fricassée

Takes 35 minutes
15 *POINTS* values per recipe
385 calories per serving

Serves 2 This recipe uses low fat soft cheese which reduces the fat but keeps the creamy taste.

100 g (3½ oz) brown rice
low fat cooking spray
2 x 125 g (4½ oz) skinless boneless chicken breasts
300 ml (10 fl oz) chicken stock
110 g (4 oz) carrots, peeled and cut into thick chunks
150 g (5½ oz) button mushrooms, sliced
1 garlic clove, crushed
75 g (2¾ oz) low fat soft cheese

1 Bring a pan of water to the boil and cook the rice according to the packet instructions. Drain well and leave to cool.
2 Meanwhile, lightly coat a deep, lidded, non stick frying pan with low fat cooking spray and heat until hot. Add the chicken and cook for 3–4 minutes until browned all over. Add the stock and carrots. Bring to the boil, cover and simmer for 10–15 minutes until tender.
3 Meanwhile, lightly coat another small non stick frying pan with low fat cooking spray. Add the mushrooms and cook, stirring, for 5 minutes until the juices have been released and evaporated. Add the garlic and rice and cook for a further minute, until hot. Divide between two plates.
4 Remove the chicken and carrots with a slotted spoon, reserving the stock. Place the chicken and carrots on top of the rice. Keep warm. Return the pan with the stock to the hob. Boil quickly for 1 minute. Remove from the heat. Stir in the soft cheese. Pour the sauce over the chicken.

Tip Try 500 g (1 lb 2 oz) pork escalopes instead of chicken for a *POINTS* value of 7½ per serving.

Rosemary lamb bake

Takes 15 minutes to prepare, 30 minutes to cook
14 *POINTS* values per recipe
390 calories per serving

Serves 2 A one pot roast, ready in under an hour, is great for midweek suppers or even a casual Sunday lunch.

200 g (7 oz) new potatoes, scrubbed and halved
200 g (7 oz) carrots, peeled and cut into chunks
1 red onion, cut into wedges
4 x 125 g (4½ oz) lamb leg steaks
2 rosemary sprigs
450 ml (16 fl oz) chicken or vegetable stock
salt and freshly ground black pepper

1 Preheat the oven to Gas Mark 6/200°C/fan oven 180°C.
2 Place the potatoes, carrots and onion in a large roasting tin. Sprinkle with a little seasoning.
3 Place the lamb steaks and rosemary on top.
4 Pour over the stock and bake for 30 minutes until golden and cooked through.

Tips You can use the same quantity of lean pork chops instead of the lamb, for a *POINTS* value of 6½ per serving.

For a change when using lamb or pork, add half a thinly sliced lemon to the vegetables – it will cook in the stock and give the juices extra flavour. The *POINTS* values will remain the same.

Goes well with: the Parsnip Purée on **page 154**, for an extra 2 *POINTS* values per serving.

food for the family

Veggie shepherd's pie

vegan ❄

Takes 35 minutes to prepare, 15 minutes to cook

15½ *POINTS* values per recipe

301 calories per serving

Serves 4 This variation of the classic pie uses Quorn mince and a lovely parsnip mash.

low fat cooking spray
2 celery sticks, chopped finely
1 leek, sliced thinly
1 x 198 g can sweetcorn, drained
500 g (1 lb 2 oz) passata
300 g (10½ oz) Quorn mince, fresh or frozen
2 teaspoons yeast extract
600 g (1 lb 5 oz) potatoes, cut into chunks
300 g (10½ oz) parsnips, peeled and cut into chunks
salt and freshly ground black pepper

1 Lightly coat a lidded non stick frying pan with low fat cooking spray and heat until hot. Add the celery and leek and stir fry for 5 minutes. Add the sweetcorn, passata, Quorn mince and yeast extract plus 300 ml (10 fl oz) water. Bring to the boil, cover and simmer for 10 minutes. Season.
2 Meanwhile, bring a large pan of water to the boil, add the potatoes and parsnips. Simmer for 15 minutes until tender. Drain, reserving 2 tablespoons of the cooking liquid, and mash. Add in the reserved cooking liquid. Season. Mix well.
3 Preheat the grill to medium. Pour the Quorn mixture into a large gratin dish, top with the mash and grill for 5–10 minutes until golden.

Serving suggestion Serve with steamed broccoli on the side, for no extra *POINTS* values.

Tip Sweet potato also makes a good topping – exchange the parsnip for the equivalent weight in sweet potato. The *POINTS* values per serving will remain the same.

Sweet and sour tofu and vegetables

vegan

Takes 20 minutes

17½ *POINTS* values per recipe

375 calories per serving

Serves 4 The tang of sweet and sour gives tofu a new lease of life in this quick stir fry.

240 g (8½ oz) brown rice
low fat cooking spray
1 onion, sliced
1 courgette, sliced thinly
1 carrot, peeled and cut into sticks
1 red pepper, deseeded and sliced
250 g (9 oz) tofu, cubed
75 g (2¾ oz) frozen peas
1 x 227 g can pineapple cubes in natural juice
3 tablespoons tomato purée
2 tablespoons white wine vinegar
2 teaspoons artificial sweetener

1 Bring a pan of water to the boil and cook the rice according to the packet instructions. Drain well and keep hot.
2 Meanwhile, lightly coat a large non stick frying pan with low fat cooking spray and heat until hot. Add the onion, courgette, carrot and pepper and stir fry for 3–4 minutes until just tender.
3 Add the tofu, peas, pineapple and juice, tomato purée, vinegar and sweetener. Cook, stirring, for 1–2 minutes until everything is hot. Serve with the brown rice.

Tip If you prefer, to serve four, cook 250 g (9 oz) noodles instead of the rice, for the same *POINTS* values per serving.

food for the family

In this chapter you'll discover how to create some exciting combinations without spending a fortune. These delicious, economical dishes are certain to become favourites. You can enjoy contemporary dishes such as Steak 'n' Jackets, Braised Lamb Shanks and Pasta Arrabiata, or recipes from around the world such as Cajun Chicken or the Swedish Jansson's Temptation and Poached Eggs.

on a
budget

Chicken livers on toast

Takes 15 minutes
6½ *POINTS* values per recipe
238 calories per serving

Serves 1 Chicken livers are tasty and take no time at all to cook. Adding some mushrooms, tomatoes and a slice of wholemeal toast makes a complete meal.

low fat cooking spray
50 g (1¾ oz) mushrooms, sliced
1 rasher smoked lean back bacon, chopped
1 garlic clove, crushed
150 g (5½ oz) whole chicken livers
1 tomato, chopped
1 medium slice wholemeal or granary bread

1 Lightly coat a non stick frying pan with low fat cooking spray and heat until hot. Add the mushrooms and bacon and stir fry for 5 minutes until the bacon is beginning to brown.
2 Add the garlic and cook for a further minute. Add the chicken livers, tomato and 2 tablespoons water. Reduce the heat and simmer for 3–4 minutes until the livers are tender.
3 Toast the slice of bread and serve the livers on top.

Tip For something more substantial, omit the toast and cook 60 g (2 oz) pasta and then toss it into the mixture, for a *POINTS* value of 8½ per serving.

Jansson's temptation and poached eggs

Takes 20 minutes to prepare, 20–30 minutes to cook
15½ *POINTS* values per recipe
266 calories per serving

Serves 4 This is a lighter version of the rich Swedish supper dish.

low fat cooking spray
1 onion, sliced thinly
2 garlic cloves, sliced
800 g (1 lb 11 oz) potatoes, peeled and cut into thin sticks
4 anchovies (25 g/1 oz), rinsed and chopped
6 tablespoons skimmed milk
4 eggs
salt and freshly ground black pepper

1 Preheat the oven to Gas Mark 6/200°C/fan oven 180°C.
2 Lightly coat a large non stick frying pan with low fat cooking spray and heat until hot. Add the onion and cook for 5 minutes until beginning to soften. Add the garlic and potatoes and stir fry for 5 minutes until everything is beginning to brown. Remove from the heat and season.
3 Transfer the potato mixture to an ovenproof dish. Scatter over the anchovies and pour in the milk. Bake for 20–30 minutes until the potato is tender and crispy. Check after 15 minutes and cover with foil if necessary.
4 Meanwhile, bring a pan of water to the boil, crack the eggs individually into a ramekin and then add to the water. Cook on a very low heat for 3 minutes before serving on top of the potatoes.

Tip Buy the exact amount of anchovies you need from the deli counter, rather than a whole jar.

on a budget

4 POINTS VALUE

Savoury pancakes

Takes 40 minutes
13½ POINTS values per recipe
209 calories per serving

Serves 4 Wholemeal flour adds a great savoury taste to these pancakes.

100 g (3½ oz) wholemeal flour
1 egg white
300 ml (10 fl oz) skimmed milk
2 teaspoons vegetable oil

for the filling
low fat cooking spray
2 onions, sliced
4 rashers lean back bacon, chopped
6 tomatoes, halved
salt and freshly ground black pepper

1   Place the flour in a bowl and make a well in the centre. Add the egg white, stirring carefully to form a batter. When the batter becomes too stiff to mix, begin adding the milk, a little at a time, until it has all been used and the batter is smooth.
2   Heat the oil in a small non stick frying pan until hot, then drain and reserve. Add a ladleful of batter, swirling it around to coat the pan. Cook for 1–2 minutes until golden underneath before flipping to cook the other side. Slide out of the pan and keep warm. Repeat to make 8 pancakes, adding a little of the reserved oil when necessary.
3   For the filling, lightly coat a non stick frying pan with low fat cooking spray and add the onions. Stir fry for 8–10 minutes over a medium heat until tender and beginning to caramelise. Add the bacon and tomatoes and cook for a further 3 minutes until everything is cooked and the tomatoes are oozing.
4   Season the filling and then divide between the pancakes. Serve hot and 2 pancakes per person.

Tips A foolproof method of making batter is to put all the ingredients in a food processor and blend until smooth.

Batter benefits from sitting for 30 minutes before cooking.

on a budget

Sardine pasta bake

Takes 30 minutes
27½ POINTS values per recipe
433 calories per serving

Serves 4 This is a great way to eat oily fish and makes a quick and easy mid week supper, since most of the ingredients come from the store cupboard.

275 g (9½ oz) pasta shapes, e.g. penne
75 g (2¾ oz) frozen sweetcorn, or canned sweetcorn, drained
2 x 120 g tins sardines in tomato sauce, mashed roughly
2 tablespoons tomato purée
150 g (5½ oz) chopped frozen spinach, defrosted
60 g (2 oz) mature Cheddar cheese, grated
salt and freshly ground black pepper

1 Bring a large pan of water to the boil, add the pasta and cook according to the packet instructions. If using frozen sweetcorn, add for the final minute of cooking to defrost it. Drain, reserving 2 tablespoons of the cooking liquid.
2 Preheat the grill to medium. Return the pasta to the pan with the cooking liquid and mix in the sardines, tomato purée, spinach and canned sweetcorn, if using. Season. Heat for 1–2 minutes until hot and then spoon into an ovenproof dish. Sprinkle with the cheese and grill for 4–5 minutes until bubbling.

Tip Try 200 g (7 oz) canned tuna instead of the sardines, for a **POINTS** value of 6 per serving.

Kale and potato soup with salami

Takes 20 minutes to prepare, 25–30 minutes to cook
5½ POINTS values per recipe
169 calories per serving

Serves 2 This interesting combination comes from Eastern Europe.

150 g (5½ oz) potatoes, peeled and diced
1 leek, sliced
2 garlic cloves, chopped
700 ml (1¼ pints) vegetable stock
75 g (2¾ oz) curly kale
40 g (1½ oz) sliced German salami, cut into strips

1 Place the potatoes, leek, garlic and stock in a large lidded saucepan. Bring to the boil, cover, reduce the heat and simmer for 20 minutes. Remove from the heat and roughly mash so that the potato forms a creamy soup.
2 Return the pan to the heat, add the kale and cook for 6–8 minutes until tender.
3 Heat a small non stick frying pan until hot. Add the strips of salami and dry fry until beginning to brown. Serve the soup garnished with the strips of salami.

Tip Curly kale tends to be a late winter vegetable. If you can't find it, substitute finely sliced cabbage instead. The **POINTS** values will remain the same.

on a budget

Mushroom and herb soufflé omelette

Ⓥ

Takes 15 minutes
2½ *POINTS* values per recipe
195 calories per serving

Serves 1 Soufflé omelettes are not difficult to make and more filling than normal ones.

low fat cooking spray
50 g (1¾ oz) mushrooms, sliced
2 spring onions, sliced
1 garlic clove, sliced
2 eggs, separated
3 tablespoons freshly chopped mixed herbs, e.g.
    parsley, chives, basil

1 Lightly coat a small non stick frying pan with low fat cooking spray and heat until hot. Add the mushrooms, spring onions and garlic and stir fry for 5 minutes until the mushrooms begin to brown.
2 Beat together the egg yolks.
3 In a clean, grease free bowl, whisk the egg whites until they hold soft peaks. Carefully fold the egg yolks into the whites together with the herbs.
4 Add the mixture to the pan, spreading it out evenly. Cook for 2–3 minutes until golden on the bottom. Fold in half and slide out of the pan to serve immediately.

Tip Try adding 25 g (1 oz) crumbled Stilton cheese to the pan on top of the egg mixture, for a *POINTS* value of 5½ per serving.

Braised lamb shanks

Takes 15 minutes to prepare, 2 hours to cook
16 *POINTS* values per recipe
315 calories per serving

Serves 2 Slow cooking makes the lamb just melt in the mouth.

low fat cooking spray
1 leek, sliced
1 onion, chopped
2 carrots, peeled and sliced
2 garlic cloves, sliced
2 x 250 g (9 oz) lamb shanks
500 ml (18 fl oz) chicken or vegetable stock
½ lemon, quartered

1 Lightly coat a large, lidded saucepan with low fat cooking spray and heat until hot. Add the leek, onion and carrots and cook over a medium heat for 5 minutes until beginning to soften.
2 Add the garlic, lamb shanks, stock and the lemon quarters. Bring to the boil, cover and simmer for 2 hours until tender.
3 Take out the lemon and discard. Skim off any excess fat on the top of the juice and serve.

Tip This is the perfect cook ahead meal – prepare it the night before, let the flavours infuse and reheat to serve the following day with 150 g (5½ oz) cooked brown rice per person, for an additional *POINTS* value of 3 per serving.

Goes well with: the Roasted Autumn Fruit Salad on **page 186**, as a dessert for an extra 1 *POINTS* value per serving.

Chermoula

Takes 15 minutes to prepare, 25 minutes to cook

5½ *POINTS* values per recipe

109 calories per serving

Serves 4 This tomato based stew with broad beans originates in North Africa.

low fat cooking spray
1 onion, sliced
200 g (7 oz) potatoes, peeled and diced
2 garlic cloves, crushed
1 teaspoon paprika
1 teaspoon ground cumin
a pinch of chilli flakes
150 ml (5 fl oz) vegetable stock
1 x 400 g can chopped tomatoes
175 g (6 oz) frozen broad beans
110 g (4 oz) frozen peas

to serve
1 tablespoon freshly chopped coriander
4 lemon wedges

1 Lightly coat a large lidded saucepan with low fat cooking spray and heat until hot. Add the onion and cook, stirring, for 5 minutes. Add the potatoes and garlic, and continue to cook for 2–3 minutes until they begin to brown. Add the spices and cook for a further minute.

2 Pour in the stock, tomatoes and broad beans. Bring to the boil and cover. Reduce the heat and cook for 20 minutes until the potato is tender. Stir in the peas and cook for a further 2 minutes until hot.

3 Serve the stew sprinkled with coriander and a lemon wedge to squeeze over.

Tip Sweet potato works well in this recipe too – replace 100 g (3½ oz) potato with 100 g (3½ oz) sweet potato. The *POINTS* values will remain the same.

Steak 'n' jackets

Takes 20 minutes to prepare, 1 hour to cook

20½ *POINTS* values per recipe

327 calories per serving

Serves 4 This meal is very convenient since it can be left to cook while you do something else.

4 x 175 g (6 oz) baking potatoes
low fat cooking spray
450 g (1 lb) casserole steak
1 red onion, sliced
150 g (5½ oz) carrots, cut in chunks
150 g (5½ oz) parsnips, cut in chunks
300 ml (10 fl oz) beef stock
1 tablespoon Worcestershire sauce

1 Preheat the oven to Gas Mark 5/190°C/fan oven 170°C. Place the potatoes on a baking tray and cook in the oven for 45 minutes to 1 hour until tender and crispy on the outside.

2 Spray a large lidded pan with low fat cooking spray and heat until hot. Add the steak and fry over a high heat until sealed on all sides. Add the vegetables, stock and Worcestershire sauce. Cover and simmer for 45 minutes. Remove the lid and continue cooking for another 15 minutes until the meat is tender.

3 Halve the potatoes and serve the meat and vegetables on top with lots of the juices.

Serving suggestion Serve with steamed cauliflower on the side, for no extra *POINTS* values.

on a budget

Chunky minestrone soup

Takes 20 minutes
6 *POINTS* values per recipe
209 calories per serving

Serves 2 This makes a filling meal and could easily be taken to work and reheated for lunch.

low fat cooking spray
1 onion, chopped
2 rashers smoked lean back bacon, chopped
110 g (4 oz) mixed frozen vegetables
1 x 227 g can chopped tomatoes
450 ml (16 fl oz) vegetable stock
50 g (1¾ oz) small pasta shapes
25 g (1 oz) cabbage, shredded, or curly kale, chopped

1 Lightly coat a large lidded pan with low fat cooking spray and heat until hot.
2 Add the onion and bacon and cook for 3–4 minutes or until tender. Add the mixed vegetables, tomatoes, stock and pasta.
3 Bring to the boil, cover and simmer for 10 minutes or until the pasta is cooked through.
4 Add the cabbage or kale and simmer for a further 5 minutes until tender. Serve in large bowls.

Tip Treat yourself with 2 teaspoons finely grated Parmesan cheese on top, for an extra 1½ *POINTS* values per serving.

Turkey with tomato and chick pea sauce

Takes 10 minutes to prepare, 25 minutes to cook
12½ *POINTS* values per recipe
210 calories per serving

Serves 4 A delicious one pot bake with turkey steaks cooked on top of an olive and garlic tomato sauce.

1 x 400 g can chopped tomatoes
1 x 410 g can chick peas, drained
30 g (1¼ oz) black olives in brine, drained and chopped
2 garlic cloves, crushed
2 teaspoons dried mixed herbs
½ chicken stock cube, dissolved in 150 ml (5 fl oz) hot water
4 x 110 g (4 oz) turkey breast steaks

1 Preheat the oven to Gas Mark 5/190°C/fan oven 170°C.
2 Mix together the tomatoes, chick peas, olives, garlic, herbs and stock. Pour into a shallow ovenproof dish or roasting tin.
3 Place the turkey steaks on top and bake for 25 minutes until the steaks are beginning to brown and then serve.

Serving suggestions Serve with four 150 g (5½ oz) jacket potatoes and steamed broccoli, for for an extra 2 *POINTS* values per serving.

Tip Try this recipe with 4 x 125 g (4½ oz) skinless boneless chicken breasts, for a *POINTS* value of 3 per serving.

on a budget

Pasta arrabiata

Ⓥ vegan (sauce only) ❄ sauce only
Takes 35 minutes
19½ *POINTS* values per recipe
390 calories per serving

Serves 4 This spicy tomato sauce is quick and easy to prepare.

low fat cooking spray
1 onion, chopped finely
1 garlic clove, crushed
1 x 400 g can chopped tomatoes
2 teaspoons dried chilli flakes
½ vegetable stock cube, crumbled
1 tablespoon tomato purée
400 g (14 oz) fusilli pasta

1 Lightly coat a lidded saucepan with low fat cooking spray and heat until hot. Add the onion and garlic and cook for 5 minutes until beginning to brown.
2 Add the tomatoes, chilli and stock cube with 100 ml (3½ fl oz) water. Cover and simmer for 10 minutes. Stir in the tomato purée.
3 Bring a large pan of water to the boil, add the pasta and cook according to the packet instructions.
4 Drain well, add the sauce to the pan and toss to mix.

Serving suggestion Serve with a zero *POINTS* value salad.

Tip You may wish to make a double quantity of this sauce and freeze it.

Salmon patties

❄
Takes 20 minutes to prepare, 15–20 minutes to cook
9 *POINTS* values per recipe
155 calories per serving

Serves 4 Making home made fish cakes with a can of salmon is quick and the result is delicious.

500 g (1 lb 2 oz) potatoes, peeled and cut into chunks
low fat cooking spray
4 spring onions, chopped
1 x 180 g can pink skinless boneless salmon, drained and flaked
1 small lemon
salt and freshly ground black pepper

1 Bring a large pan of water to the boil, add the potatoes and simmer for 15–20 minutes until tender. Drain well and then mash.
2 Lightly coat a non stick frying pan with low fat cooking spray and heat until sizzling. Add the spring onions and cook for 2–3 minutes until wilted and beginning to brown. Mix into the mash together with the salmon.
3 Finely grate the zest of the lemon, stir into the mixture and season. Cut the remaining lemon into wedges and set aside.
4 When cool enough to handle, shape into eight small patties or into four larger ones.
5 Spray the frying pan again with low fat cooking spray and heat until hot. Add the patties and cook for 5 minutes, turning carefully every now and then until golden on both sides.
6 Serve with the lemon wedges.

Serving suggestion Serve with a zero *POINTS* value salad.

Goes well with: the Fresh Tomato Salsa on **page 198**, for no extra *POINTS* values.

on a budget

Cajun chicken

Takes 15 minutes to prepare, 25 minutes to cook

16 *POINTS* values per recipe

425 calories per serving

Serves 2 Chicken drumsticks dusted with Cajun spices make a tasty meal.

2 teaspoons Cajun spice

4 x 75 g (2¾ oz) skinless chicken drumsticks

low fat cooking spray

125 g (4½ oz) couscous

150 ml (5 fl oz) chicken stock

40 g (1½ oz) peas, defrosted

1 x 198 g can sweetcorn, drained

2 spring onions, chopped

zest and juice 1 lime

salt and freshly ground black pepper

1 Preheat the oven to Gas Mark 6/200°C/fan oven 180°C.

2 Sprinkle the spice over the drumsticks, ensuring they are evenly coated. Spray generously with low fat cooking spray and bake in a roasting pan for 25 minutes until golden and cooked through. When a skewer is inserted, the juices should run clear.

3 Place the couscous and stock in a lidded pan and bring to the boil. Take off the heat, cover with a tight fitting lid and leave to steam. After 10 minutes, fluff up the couscous with a fork and stir in the peas, sweetcorn, spring onions, lime zest and juice. Season.

4 Serve the drumsticks on a bed of the couscous.

Tip If you prefer, cook all the ingredients, leave to cool and chill to enjoy as a salad. It makes a great lunch box too.

Beef and mushroom fried rice

Takes 30 minutes

19½ *POINTS* values per recipe

273 calories per serving

Serves 4 The economy packs of mushrooms available in supermarkets are ideal for this recipe.

150 g (5½ oz) wholegrain brown rice

300 g (10½ oz) lean minced beef

low fat cooking spray

250 g (9 oz) mushrooms, sliced if large

2 garlic cloves, crushed

110 g (4 oz) beansprouts

60 g (2 oz) dark green cabbage, shredded finely

1 egg, beaten

2 tablespoons soy sauce

salt and freshly ground black pepper

1 Bring a large pan of water to the boil, add the rice and cook according to the packet instructions. Drain.

2 Meanwhile, heat a wok or non stick frying pan until hot, add the beef and stir fry for 8–10 minutes until crispy – you will need to do this at a high heat. Remove from the pan, season and set aside. Keep warm.

3 Lightly coat the same pan with low fat cooking spray, add the mushrooms and cook for 5–7 minutes until the juices have evaporated and the mushrooms are beginning to brown. Add the garlic, beansprouts and cabbage. Stir fry for 2–3 minutes until the cabbage is wilted, then add the rice, egg and soy sauce. Cook, stirring, for 1–2 minutes until hot and the egg is cooked.

4 Serve the rice on hot plates topped with the crispy beef.

on a budget

These vegetarian recipes are truly inspiring and you'll discover new combinations using ingredients which are readily available as well as easy to prepare. Try the Spicy Veggie Chilli with Tortilla Chips or stove top Lentil and Chick Pea Casserole. If you want to impress your guests, how about the Asparagus and Basil Tart, the all-in-one-pan Roasted Ragoût with Borlotti Beans or the summery Courgette and Pesto Pasta with Halloumi. All are incredibly delicious.

vegetarian

Baked aubergine rounds

Takes 20 minutes to prepare, 15–20 minutes to cook

3½ *POINTS* values per recipe

148 calories per serving

Serves 2 These crispy aubergine rounds are delicious.

1 small aubergine, sliced into 12 rounds
40 g (1½ oz) polenta
1 teaspoon mixed dried herbs
1 garlic clove, crushed
1 egg, beaten
low fat cooking spray
salt and freshly ground black pepper
mixed salad leaves, to serve

for the salsa
1 tomato on the vine, deseeded and diced
4 cm (1½ inches) piece cucumber, diced
1 spring onion, sliced thinly
1 tablespoon chopped parsley
juice of ½ lime

1 Preheat the oven to Gas Mark 6/200°C/fan oven 180°C. Line a baking tray with non stick baking parchment. To make the salsa, combine all the ingredients and chill until ready to serve.

2 Heat a non stick griddle or non stick frying pan until hot and cook the aubergine slices for 1–2 minutes, turning once, until beginning to char. Set aside. You may have to do this in batches.

3 Mix together the polenta, herbs and garlic and season. Dip the aubergine slices first into the egg and then into the polenta, coating both sides. Place on the baking tray and spray with low fat cooking spray. Bake for 15–20 minutes until golden.

4 Serve the baked rounds on mixed salad leaves and a dollop of the salsa on the side.

Spanakopita

Takes 35 minutes to prepare, 25–30 minutes to cook

8½ *POINTS* values per recipe

321 calories per serving

Serves 2 This Greek dish is equally good hot or cold.

low fat cooking spray
1 onion, sliced thinly
2 garlic cloves, crushed
300 g (10½ oz) spinach
a kettle full of boiling water
50 g (1¾ oz) reduced fat feta cheese, cubed
1 egg, beaten
½ teaspoon caraway seeds
8 x 14 g sheets filo pastry (30 cm x 18 cm/12 inches x 7 inches)
salt and freshly ground black pepper

1 Lightly coat a non stick frying pan with low fat cooking spray and heat until hot. Add the onion, reduce the heat and cook for 10 minutes until beginning to brown. Stir in the garlic and cook for a further 2 minutes. Remove from the heat.

2 Preheat the oven to Gas Mark 6/200°C/fan oven 180°C. Place the spinach in a colander and pour over boiling water. Drain, cool and squeeze out any excess liquid with the back of a wooden spoon before chopping roughly.

3 Mix the spinach and onions together with the feta cheese, egg and caraway seeds. Season.

4 Spray a sheet of filo with low fat cooking spray and lay on a baking tray. Spray another and lay it beside the first, but just overlapping, to make a square. Repeat with two more sheets, laying them the opposite way, but on top. Place the spinach mixture in the middle and spread to within 5 cm (2 inches) of the edge. Fold up the edges and then top with two more sheets of sprayed filo. Seal the edges. Repeat with two more sheets and then spray the whole thing before baking for 25–30 minutes until golden.

Potato, mushroom and thyme fritters

Takes 25 minutes

7 *POINTS* values per recipe

222 calories per serving

Serves 2 Delicious low fat fritters.

low fat cooking spray
110 g (4 oz) button mushrooms, halved if large
1 garlic clove, crushed
50 g (1¾ oz) self raising flour
1 egg
3 tablespoons skimmed milk
150 g (5½ oz) potatoes, grated
2 teaspoons chopped fresh thyme leaves
salt and freshly ground black pepper
2 tablespoons ready made tomato relish, to serve

1 Lightly coat a non stick frying pan with low fat cooking spray. Heat until hot. Add the mushrooms and cook, stirring, for 5–7 minutes. Add the garlic. Cook for 1 minute. Remove the mushrooms and garlic from the pan and set aside.

2 Sift the flour into a large bowl, make a well in the centre and crack the egg into it. Gradually mix together, drawing the flour into the middle as you stir. Once the mixture gets too thick to incorporate any more flour, begin adding the milk, a little at a time, until you have a thick, smooth batter.

3 Use your hands to squeeze out as much liquid as possible from the potatoes. Stir into the batter with the mushrooms, garlic and thyme. Season.

4 Clean the frying pan and lightly coat again with low fat cooking spray. Heat until hot, then place spoonfuls of the mixture into the pan. (You may need to do this in batches.) Cook for 1–2 minutes until golden underneath before turning. The fritters should puff up. Serve hot with the relish.

Serving suggestion Serve with a zero *POINTS* value green salad.

Asparagus and basil tart

Takes 15 minutes to prepare, 20 minutes to cook

10 *POINTS* values per recipe

420 calories per serving

Serves 2 This makes a lovely summer lunch and is best eaten the day it's made.

450 g (1 lb) fine asparagus, trimmed
low fat cooking spray
2 onions, chopped finely
6 x 14 g sheets filo pastry (30 cm x 18 cm/12 inches x 7 inches)
2 eggs, beaten
salt and freshly ground black pepper

to serve
2 tablespoon pine nuts, toasted
a handful of basil leaves

1 Preheat the oven to Gas Mark 5/190°C/fan oven 170°C. Bring a large pan of water to the boil. Place a steamer over the pan. Add the asparagus. Cook for 3–5 minutes until just tender. (If you don't have a steamer, cook it in a small amount of boiling water.) Remove from the heat and plunge into cold water to stop it cooking further.

2 Lightly coat a pan with low fat cooking spray and heat until hot. Add the onions and cook over a low heat until beginning to caramelise, about 8–10 minutes. Set aside to cool slightly.

3 Spray a sheet of filo pastry with low fat cooking spray. Use to line a 30 x 20 cm (12 x 8 inch) Swiss roll tin. Repeat the layering of the pastry, using the low fat cooking spray and all the sheets.

4 Mix together the onion and eggs, and season. Spread over the filo pastry. Top with the asparagus spears, lining them up neatly. Bake for 20 minutes until the pastry is golden and the egg mixture set. Serve garnished with the pine nuts and basil leaves.

vegetarian

Crunchy veggie patties

Y

Takes 10 minutes to prepare, 20–25 minutes to cook

4½ *POINTS* values per recipe

82 calories per serving

Serves 4 These make a tasty base for a salad and are similar to rosti.

75 g (2¾ oz) carrots, peeled and grated
75 g (2¾ oz) courgette, grated
40 g (1½ oz) wholemeal breadcrumbs
1 egg, beaten
2 teaspoons poppy seeds
1 tablespoon snipped chives
10 g (¼ oz) freshly grated Parmesan
salt and freshly ground black pepper
mixed green salad, to serve

1 Preheat the oven to Gas Mark 6/ 200°C/fan oven 180°C. Line a baking tray with non stick baking parchment.

2 Combine all the ingredients in a bowl and season. Shape into four patties, place on the baking tray and press down until flat.

3 Bake for 20–25 minutes until golden and crispy. Cool slightly on the baking tray.

4 To serve, pile the salad on to the patties.

Tip Try adding some spices. 1 teaspoon cumin works well with the carrot in place of the poppy seeds.

Spicy veggie chilli with tortilla chips

Y **vegan without the yogurt** ❋ **chilli only**

Takes 20 minutes to prepare, 20 minutes to cook

7½ *POINTS* values per recipe

329 calories per serving

Serves 2 Delicious with home made tortilla chips.

low fat cooking spray
1 onion, chopped
2 garlic cloves, chopped
1 red chilli, deseeded and diced
75 g (2¾ oz) mushrooms, sliced
75 g (2¾ oz) Quorn mince
1 x 400 g can chopped tomatoes
200 ml (7 fl oz) vegetable stock
1 teaspoon yeast extract
1 x 410 g can kidney beans, drained
1 pitta bread, split and cut into 16 triangles
1 teaspoon smoked paprika
salt

to serve
2 tablespoons 0% fat Greek yogurt
1 tablespoon freshly chopped parsley

1 Lightly coat a lidded non stick frying pan with low fat cooking spray. Heat until hot. Add the onion. Cook for 5 minutes until softened. Add the garlic, chilli and mushrooms. Stir fry for 2 minutes.

2 Add the Quorn mince, tomatoes, stock and yeast extract. Bring to the boil, cover and simmer for 15 minutes. Add the kidney beans and cook for a further 5 minutes.

3 To make the tortilla chips, preheat the oven to Gas Mark 6/200°C/fan oven 180°C. Spread the pitta triangles over a baking tray, spray with low fat cooking spray, dust with paprika and a little salt. Bake for 5–8 minutes until golden and crispy.

4 Serve each plate with a tablespoon of yogurt, a sprinkle of parsley, and the tortillas on the side.

vegetarian

Spinach Scotch pancakes

  pancakes only

Takes 20 minutes
12 *POINTS* values per recipe
426 calories per serving

Serves 2 A great supper or brunch dish.

110 g (4 oz) self raising flour
1 egg
100 ml (3½ fl oz) skimmed milk
110 g (4 oz) frozen chopped spinach, defrosted,
    drained and excess water squeezed out
low fat cooking spray
4 Quorn bacon style rashers
2 eggs
salt and freshly ground black pepper

1 Place the flour in a large bowl, make a well in the centre and add the egg. Use a wooden spoon to mix carefully, drawing in the flour. Gradually add the milk to make a thick smooth batter. Stir in the spinach and season.
2 Lightly coat a non stick frying pan with low fat cooking spray and heat until hot. Place spoonfuls of the mixture in the pan (you should have enough to make four pancakes), leaving room for them to spread. Cook for 1–2 minutes until beginning to brown underneath, then turn and cook for a further 1–2 minutes. Set aside and keep warm.
3 Spray the pan again and cook the Quorn rashers for 1 minute on each side until golden.
4 Bring a large shallow pan of water to the boil and then let it simmer. Crack 1 egg into a ramekin. Swirl the simmering water in the pan and while doing so, carefully add the egg to the pan. This will bring the egg white into a rounded shape. Repeat with the second egg. Cook the eggs for 3 minutes, then remove with a slotted spoon.
5 Serve two pancakes each, topped with a poached egg and two Quorn rashers.

Courgette and pesto pasta with halloumi

Takes 30 minutes
23½ *POINTS* values per recipe
399 calories per serving

Serves 4 This is a lovely summer pasta dish which uses the Greek cheese halloumi.

240 g (8½ oz) dried conchiglie pasta
2 courgettes, cut into ribbons (see Tip)
low fat cooking spray
175 g (6 oz) halloumi, cut into thin slices
3 tablespoons reduced fat pesto
a handful of basil leaves, to garnish

1 Bring a large pan of water to the boil, add the pasta and cook according to the packet instructions. Drain, reserving 4 tablespoons of cooking liquid.
2 Meanwhile, heat a griddle or non stick frying pan until hot. Spray the courgette ribbons with low fat cooking spray and cook for 1–2 minutes, turning once until charred and just cooked. You may have to do this in batches.
3 Spray the pieces of halloumi with low fat cooking spray and cook in the frying pan for 2–3 minutes, turning once, until golden.
4 Return the pasta to the pan with the reserved cooking liquid, courgette ribbons and the pesto. Stir to combine and heat gently for 2–3 minutes until hot. Serve the pasta in large bowls topped with the halloumi and some basil leaves to garnish.

Tip Use a vegetable peeler to cut ribbons of courgette.

Goes well with: the Parma Ham Bruschetta on **page 36**, as a starter for an extra 4½ *POINTS* values per serving.

vegetarian

Spicy Quorn and bean pie

Takes 45 minutes
20 *POINTS* values per recipe
372 calories per serving

Serves 4 This is easy to make and a family favourite – ideal for a Bonfire Night party.

800 g (1 lb 11 oz) potatoes, cut into chunks
low fat cooking spray
1 leek, chopped finely
350 g (12 oz) Quorn chicken style pieces
1 x 410 g can reduced sugar and salt baked beans
1 x 198 g can sweetcorn, drained
1 tablespoon mild chilli powder
1 chicken stock cube, crumbled
6 cherry tomatoes, halved
salt and freshly ground black pepper

1 Bring a large pan of water to the boil, add the potatoes and cook for 15 minutes until tender. Drain and mash.
2 Meanwhile, lightly coat a medium non stick frying pan with low fat cooking spray and heat until hot. Add the chopped leek and stir fry for 5–7 minutes until tender and beginning to brown. Add to the mash and season. Re-spray the frying pan with low fat cooking spray and heat until hot. Add the Quorn pieces and stir fry for 3–5 minutes until beginning to brown.
3 Place the beans, sweetcorn, chilli powder, Quorn pieces and stock cube in a pan over a low heat and heat for 2–3 minutes until hot. Preheat the grill to medium.
4 Pour the bean mixture into an ovenproof dish and top with the mash. Decorate with the tomatoes and grill for 5–10 minutes until golden.

Serving suggestion Serve with steamed broccoli for no extra *POINTS* values.

Creamy bulgar mushrooms

Takes 30 minutes
8 *POINTS* values per recipe
316 calories per serving

Serves 2 Bulgar wheat has a lovely nutty flavour.

low fat cooking spray
4 large field mushrooms, sliced
1 onion, cut into wedges
2 garlic cloves, sliced
110 g (4 oz) bulgar wheat
600 ml (1 pint) vegetable stock
50 g (1¾ oz) broccoli florets
1 tablespoon mushroom ketchup (optional)
2 tablespoons freshly chopped parsley
3 tablespoons low fat soft cheese
salt and freshly ground black pepper

1 Lightly coat a lidded non stick frying pan with low fat cooking spray and heat until hot. Add the mushrooms and onion and stir fry for 5 minutes. Add the garlic and cook for a further 2 minutes.
2 Add the bulgar wheat and stock and bring to the boil. Cover with a tight fitting lid and cook for 5 minutes. Then add the broccoli and cook for a further 5 minutes until the bulgar is cooked, the stock has been absorbed and the broccoli is tender.
3 Stir in the mushroom ketchup, if using, parsley and low fat soft cheese, and season.

Tip Dried mushrooms work well in this recipe. Use 25 g (1 oz) porcini or mixed dried mushrooms in place of the fresh, soaking them according to the packet instructions and using the soaking water in place of some of the stock. The *POINTS* values will remain the same.

vegetarian

Roasted ragoût with borlotti beans

Ⓥ vegan

Takes 10 minutes to prepare, 55 minutes to cook

3½ POINTS values per recipe

143 calories per serving

Serves 4 This is a very easy, all in one pan recipe.

1 small courgette, trimmed and cut into chunks

1 yellow pepper, deseeded and sliced

1 red pepper, deseeded and sliced

2 red onions, cut into wedges

4 garlic cloves, unpeeled

1 rosemary sprig

low fat cooking spray

10 tomatoes on the vine

1 x 410 g can borlotti beans, drained

150 ml (5 fl oz) vegetable stock

salt and freshly ground black pepper

a handful of basil leaves, to garnish

1 Preheat the oven to Gas Mark 6/200°C/fan oven 180°C.

2 Place the courgette, peppers, onions, garlic and rosemary in a large roasting tin. Spray with low fat cooking spray and cook in the oven for 30 minutes until beginning to char.

3 Add the tomatoes and cook for a further 15 minutes until they are soft.

4 Stir in the borlotti beans and stock, splitting some of the tomatoes so that they form a sauce. Cover with foil and cook for a further 10 minutes until hot.

5 Season and garnish with basil leaves before serving.

Tip Replace the borlotti beans with a drained 410 g can of green lentils, for the same **POINTS** values.

Lentil and chick pea casserole

vegan ❄

Takes 30 minutes

8½ *POINTS* values per recipe

160 calories per serving

Serves 4 This is a hearty casserole, cooked on top of the stove, containing lentils and spinach.

low fat cooking spray
1 red onion, sliced thinly
2 garlic cloves, crushed
2 celery sticks, chopped
1 teaspoon cumin seed
1 x 400 g can cherry tomatoes
1 x 410 g can green lentils, drained
1 x 410 g can chick peas, drained
1 vegetable stock cube, crumbled
150 g (5½ oz) young leaf spinach
1 tablespoon freshly chopped parsley, to garnish

1 Lightly coat a large lidded non stick saucepan with low fat cooking spray. Heat until hot. Add the onion and fry for 3 minutes. Add the garlic, celery and cumin and continue cooking in the onion juices for 3 minutes to soften the vegetables.

2 Add the tomatoes, lentils and chick peas with the stock cube and 150 ml (5 fl oz) water. Bring to the boil, cover and simmer for 10 minutes.

3 Stir in the spinach and cook for a further 2–3 minutes until the spinach has wilted. Serve hot with a sprinkle of parsley on top.

Serving suggestion Serve with 1 tablespoon of 0% fat Greek yogurt per serving, for an additional *POINTS* value of ½ per serving.

Tip If you like curry flavours, add 1 tablespoon mild curry powder with the cumin seeds. The *POINTS* values will remain the same.

vegetarian

Spicy sweet potato cakes

Ⓥ vegan ❄

Takes 25 minutes to prepare, 15 minutes to cook

3 _POINTS_ values per recipe

159 calories per serving

Serves 2 Mixing sweet potatoes with white mashed potatoes makes the cakes hold together better.

150 g (5½ oz) floury potatoes, peeled and chopped

110 g (4 oz) sweet potatoes, peeled and chopped

low fat cooking spray

½ red onion, chopped finely

1 garlic clove, crushed

1 teaspoon chilli flakes

salt and freshly ground black pepper

for the tomato sauce

1 x 227 g can chopped tomatoes with herbs

½ small red onion, diced

1 ready roasted red pepper, drained and chopped

1 Bring a large lidded pan of water to the boil. Add the potatoes and sweet potatoes. Bring to the boil, cover and simmer for 15 minutes until tender. Drain well and mash.

2 Spray a non stick frying pan with low fat cooking spray and heat until hot. Add the onion and garlic and stir fry for 2 minutes before adding the chilli and cooking for a further 1 minute. Add to the mashed potato and season well.

3 Shape the mixture into four patties. Spray the frying pan again with low fat cooking spray and heat until hot. Add the patties and cook for 5 minutes, turning once until golden on both sides. Set aside and keep warm.

4 For the sauce, place all the ingredients in a small pan and boil rapidly for 3 minutes. Serve the hot cakes with the tomato sauce.

Serving suggestion Serve with a zero **_POINTS_** value side salad.

Tip To freeze, open freeze the uncooked potato cakes until solid and then place in a freezer bag wrapped in greaseproof paper. Defrost thoroughly before cooking.

Goes well with: the Strawberry Mousses on **page 182**, as a dessert for an extra 1 **_POINTS_** value per serving.

Entertaining can be easy with these recipes. They are impressive and low in **POINTS** values. Split into starters, main courses and side dishes, you'll find a mixture of simple, yet classic combinations to enjoy, such as Warm Goat's Cheese Salad and Tapas Plates, followed by Lemon Salmon en Croûte, Duck à l'Orange and Creamy Mushroom Pork, served with Sesame and Orange Roasted Carrots and a range of vegetable purées. It will have your guests coming back for more.

entertaining

Warm goat's cheese salad

Takes 15 minutes

5 *POINTS* values per recipe

157 calories per serving

Serves 2 Lightly grilled creamy goat's cheese goes exceptionally well with the slightly sweet and sour taste of pomegranate.

½ pomegranate

2 teaspoons white or regular balsamic vinegar

a pinch of artificial sweetener

2 x 40 g (1½ oz) slices medium fat goat's cheese with rind

4 cm (1½ inches) piece cucumber, diced

6 Little Gem lettuce leaves, shredded

4 cherry tomatoes, halved

a handful of rocket leaves

1 Remove around 20 seeds from the pomegranate and reserve. Press the remaining seeds still inside the shell over a lemon squeezer to extract the juice (see Tip). Sieve to remove any bits. Mix the juice with the vinegar and sweetener.

2 Preheat the grill to medium. Place the goat's cheese slices on a piece of foil and grill for 3–4 minutes until softened.

3 Arrange the cucumber, lettuce, tomatoes and rocket on two serving plates and top each with a slice of goat's cheese. Scatter over the reserved pomegranate seeds and drizzle with the dressing. Serve at once.

Tips If you don't have a lemon squeezer, remove the red or pink pomegranate flesh and press the seeds through a metal sieve using the end of a rolling pin. Be careful, though, since they do squirt.

This can be made into a main course salad by increasing the goat's cheese to 100 g (3½ oz) per person, for a *POINTS* value of 6 per serving. You can increase the amount of leaves and tomatoes without adding any extra *POINTS* value.

The salad will taste the same with regular balsamic vinegar but it discolours the cheese. White balsamic makes the salad look better when entertaining.

2½
POINTS
VALUE

Tapas plates

Takes 15 minutes + 1 hour marinating
12 *POINTS* values per recipe
171 calories per serving

Serves 4 Spanish tapas typically consists of lots of little dishes. These are easily assembled and can be prepared in advance and then thrown together at the last minute.

110 g (4 oz) chorizo, cut into 12 pieces
4 slices Serrano ham

for the marinated olives
12 black olives in brine, drained, stoned and halved
1 teaspoon olive oil
1 tablespoon orange juice
½ teaspoon cumin seeds

for the marinated artichokes
1 x 400 g can artichokes in water, drained
zest and juice 1 lemon
1 teaspoon dried oregano

for the dip
4 tablespoons fat free fromage frais
1 garlic clove, crushed
1 tablespoon finely chopped parsley

1 Combine all the ingredients for the marinated olives, cover and set aside for 1 hour.
2 Combine all the ingredients for the marinated artichokes, cover and set aside for 1 hour.
3 To make the dip, combine all the ingredients, cover and chill until required.
4 Heat a small non stick frying pan and dry fry the chorizo pieces for 2–3 minutes until beginning to colour.
5 Place the tapas, including the chorizo and Serrano ham, on individual serving plates or bowls. Place the dip on the side for dipping and let people help themselves.

Tips You can marinate the olives and artichokes overnight in the fridge if preferred.

Buy your chorizo sausage at the deli counter, instead of ready sliced, so that you can cut it into pieces.

Mini meatballs with spicy dipping sauce

❄ meatballs only

Takes 45 minutes

7 POINTS values per recipe

89 calories per serving

Serves 4 These make great party nibbles or you can serve them as a starter to share for an informal dinner.

for the meatballs
200 g (7 oz) lean steak mince
2 tablespoons snipped chives
2 tablespoons finely chopped fresh parsley
1 egg white
low fat cooking spray
salt and freshly ground black pepper

for the dipping sauce
1 x 227 g can chopped tomatoes with garlic
2 tablespoons tomato purée
1 teaspoon chilli powder

1 In a bowl, mix together the mince, chives, parsley and egg white until well combined. Season. Shape into 12 equal sized balls.

2 Lightly coat a non stick frying pan with low fat cooking spray and heat until hot. Add the meatballs and cook, turning occasionally, for 8–10 minutes until browned and cooked through (you may need to do this in batches – keep all the meatballs warm as you do so).

3 Combine the sauce ingredients and heat in a small pan for 2–3 minutes until hot.

4 Serve the meatballs with cocktail sticks for dipping into the sauce.

Tip For a main course for two, serve the hot meatballs and sauce on top of 300 g (10½ oz) cooked pasta, for a **POINTS** value of 5½ per serving.

Parma ham and pear salad

Takes 10 minutes

4 POINTS values per recipe

102 calories per serving

Serves 2 A quick and attractive starter.

1 ripe pear
low fat cooking spray
40 g (1½ oz) watercress
4 slices Parma ham

for the dressing
zest and juice ½ lemon
2 teaspoons wholegrain mustard

1 Halve and core the pear and cut into six or eight wedges. Heat a griddle or non stick frying pan until hot. Spray the wedges all over with low fat cooking spray and cook for 2–3 minutes until beginning to char.

2 Arrange the watercress and ham on two serving plates. Top with the pear wedges.

3 Mix together the lemon zest, juice and mustard and drizzle over the salad before serving.

Tip Apple works equally well in this recipe, for a **POINTS** value of 1½ per serving.

Leek and potato rosti with smoked salmon

Takes 30 minutes
6 *POINTS* values per recipe
94 calories per serving

Serves 4 Crisp fried potato and leeks topped with a slice of smoked salmon make a delicious starter.

200 g (7 oz) potatoes, grated
1 small leek, shredded finely
low fat cooking spray
110 g (4 oz) smoked salmon
4 tablespoons 0% fat Greek yogurt
2 teaspoons chopped dill
salt and freshly ground black pepper

1 Squeeze as much liquid as you can from the potatoes, then pat dry with kitchen paper. Mix with the leek and season.
2 Lightly coat a non stick frying pan with low fat cooking spray and heat until hot. Place spoonfuls of the rosti mixture in the pan and flatten as much as possible with the back of a spatula.
3 Cook for 5–8 minutes, turning occasionally, until golden and crispy on both sides. Make eight rosti in total, which you may need to do in batches.
4 Top the rosti with slices of smoked salmon. Mix together the yogurt and dill, season with black pepper (the salmon will make it salty enough) and drizzle over the top and serve.

Tips Make 16 small rosti, dividing the topping equally, to serve as appetisers with drinks, for a *POINTS* value of ½ per rosti.

Dill and salmon go very well together, but you could use 1 teaspoon of lemon zest, instead of the dill, if you prefer.

Chicken and duck terrine

Takes 30 minutes to prepare, 1½ hours to cook +
overnight chilling

43 *POINTS* values per recipe

287 calories per serving

Serves 8 Although this is a terrine, it makes a
great dinner party main course when served with
a zero *POINTS* value salad and 110 g (4 oz) hot
new potatoes per serving, for a *POINTS* value of 1
per serving. It's not difficult and the end result is
impressive.

2 x 150 g (5½ oz) skinless boneless chicken breasts
2 x 150 g (5½ oz) skinless boneless duck breasts
100 ml (3½ fl oz) port
250 g (9 oz) lean pork mince
2 tablespoons freshly chopped tarragon
zest 1 small orange
1 egg
1 egg white
25 g (1 oz) green or black olives, in brine, drained and
   chopped
12 rashers smoked streaky bacon
125 g (4½ oz) whole cooked sweet peppers from a jar,
   drained and cut into strips
low fat cooking spray
salt and freshly ground black pepper

1 Cut the chicken breasts and one of the duck
breasts into four equal strips. Place in a non
metallic dish and marinate in the port for 10
minutes.

2 Cut the remaining duck breast into small
pieces. Place in a bowl with the pork mince,
tarragon, orange zest, eggs and olives. Mix well
and season.

3 Preheat the oven to Gas Mark 2/150°C/fan oven
130°C. Line a 900 g (2 lb) loaf tin with the bacon
rashers, ensuring they meet and overlap on the

base and overhang the edges enough to cover the
contents. You don't need to cover the ends of the
tin.

4 Drain the chicken and duck breasts, pouring any
excess marinade into the pork mixture and mixing
well. Spoon half the pork mixture into the tin. Lay
the chicken and duck pieces on top, pressing down
to level the surface. Arrange the strips of pepper
evenly over the surface and spread with the
remaining pork mixture.

5 Fold the overhanging bacon rashers over the
top. Spray some foil with low fat cooking spray and
use to cover the loaf tin, sprayed side down. Place
on a baking tray and bake for 1½ hours.

6 Remove from the oven and pour off about half
the liquid in the tin around the terrine. Cool, then
chill overnight with weights (use cans) on top to
press it down.

7 Serve cold or reheat in a microwave until piping
hot.

Tips Store in the fridge, wrapped in clingfilm for
up to 5 days or wrap and freeze.

Duck breasts are expensive so you could replace
them with chicken breasts, for a *POINTS* value of 5
per serving, although the flavour will not be quite
so gamey.

Thyme works equally well as tarragon in this
recipe.

Individual portions can be used for a lunchbox.

5½
POINTS
VALUE®

Lemon salmon en croûte

Takes 20 minutes to prepare, 25–30 minutes to cook
26 *POINTS* values per recipe
364 calories per serving

Serves 4 Individual parcels are always impressive to serve up and these are quick to make.

1 x 250 g tub low fat soft cheese
1 tablespoon each freshly chopped dill and parsley
zest and juice 1 lemon
8 x 14 g sheets filo pastry
low fat cooking spray
4 x 110 g (4 oz) salmon fillets, skinned
salt and freshly ground black pepper

1 Preheat the oven to Gas Mark 5/190°C/fan oven 170°C. Line a baking tray with non stick baking parchment.
2 Mix the low fat soft cheese with the herbs, lemon juice and zest and season.
3 Spray a sheet of filo pastry with low fat cooking spray and top with another sheet. Place a piece of salmon in the middle and top with a quarter of the cheese mixture. Fold over the edges like a parcel and spray with low fat cooking spray. Transfer to the baking tray. Repeat to make four parcels.
4 Bake for 25–30 minutes until the salmon is cooked through and the pastry golden.

Tips Make these parcels up to 2 hours in advance and refrigerate.

If you have time, marinate the salmon in the lemon juice and herbs for 30 minutes beforehand, mixing any remaining marinade with the soft cheese.

Lemon and honey lamb steaks

Takes 35 minutes to prepare + 20 minutes marinating
17½ *POINTS* values per recipe
247 calories per serving

Serves 4 Marinating these steaks for as little as 20 minutes makes them incredibly flavourful.

4 x 125 g (4½ oz) lean lamb leg steaks
zest and juice 1 small lemon
1 tablespoon runny honey
450 g (1 lb) new potatoes
2 lemon thyme sprigs
salt and freshly ground black pepper

1 Place the lamb in a non metallic bowl. Mix together the lemon zest and juice with the honey and pour over the lamb ensuring it is thoroughly coated. Set aside, uncovered, to marinate for 20 minutes.
2 Bring a pan of water to the boil, add the potatoes and simmer for 10–15 minutes until tender. Reserve 2 tablespoons of the potato cooking liquid, then drain the potatoes and lightly crush them using the back of a spoon. Add the reserved cooking liquid, lemon thyme leaves and a little seasoning. Keep warm.
3 Preheat the grill to medium. Remove the lamb from the marinade and grill for 8–10 minutes, turning once, until cooked through and beginning to char.
4 In a saucepan, boil the remaining marinade for 1 or 2 minutes, until thickened.
5 Serve the lamb with the marinade drizzled over and accompanied by the potatoes.

Serving suggestion Serve with green beans, for no extra *POINTS* values.

Tip Lemon thyme looks similar to ordinary thyme but has a fresh lemon flavour. If you can't find them, use the ordinary thyme instead.

4 1/2 POINTS VALUE ®

Beef Wellington

Takes 40 minutes
22½ POINTS values per recipe
341 calories per serving

Serves 4 Tender beef fillet wrapped in filo pastry with a quick mushroom pâté makes an impressive dinner party main course.

400 g (14 oz) beef fillet
low fat cooking spray
200 g (7 oz) mushrooms, chopped finely
2 shallots, chopped finely
150 g (5½ oz) low fat soft cheese
1 tablespoon freshly chopped tarragon
12 x 14 g sheets filo pastry
salt and freshly ground black pepper

1 Preheat the oven to Gas Mark 7/220°C/fan oven 200°C.
2 Cut the beef into four equal portions and season. Lightly coat a non stick frying pan with low fat cooking spray and heat until hot. Add the meat and cook for 3–4 minutes until browned all over. Remove from the pan and set aside.
3 Spray the pan again with low fat cooking spray and add the mushrooms and shallots. Cook, stirring, for 10 minutes over a medium heat until the mushroom juices have been released and evaporated.
4 Place the soft cheese in a bowl and beat until smooth. Add the mushroom mixture and tarragon and mix well.
5 Lightly coat a baking tray with low fat cooking spray.
6 Lay one sheet of filo pastry on a board and spray with low fat cooking spray. Add another sheet and spray that, topping with a final sheet. Place a piece of beef in the middle of the sheets, spoon on a quarter of the mushroom mixture and wrap up. You can either do this neatly, as you would wrap a parcel, or bring up the sides

and scrunch the top, making sure you seal in the contents. Carefully place on the baking tray and spray with low fat cooking spray. Repeat to make four parcels.
7 Bake the parcels for 10 minutes until the pastry is golden and crispy.

Serving suggestion Serve with steamed green beans, for no additional **POINTS** values.

Tips You can freeze this dish (if the pastry was originally frozen, it can only be frozen once the pastry has been cooked). Bake, cool and wrap in foil. Defrost overnight in the fridge before reheating in an oven preheated to Gas Mark 6/200°C/fan oven 180°C for 10 minutes until piping hot.

Filo pastry is relatively easy to use and following these tips will help: keep the pastry covered with cling film to prevent it from drying out. Handle it carefully as it is quite fragile. Remove from the fridge at least 30 minutes before use to allow it to come to room temperature – it will be more flexible that way.

Roasted vegetables with Brie and wine sauce

Takes 15 minutes to prepare, 40 minutes to cook

11½ *POINTS* values per recipe

347 calories per serving

Serves 2 A superb treat.

6 spring onions

1 fennel bulb, cut into chunks

2 pieces white chicory, halved lengthways

6 baby carrots, trimmed

2 banana shallots or large regular shallots, halved

150 g (5½ oz) new potatoes, scrubbed

2 thyme sprigs

4 garlic cloves, unpeeled

low fat cooking spray

110 g (4 oz) Brie, chopped roughly

3 tablespoons white wine

2 teaspoons fresh thyme leaves

freshly ground black pepper

1 Preheat the oven to Gas Mark 6/200°C/fan oven 180°C. Place all the vegetables in a large roasting tin with the thyme sprigs and garlic and spray the vegetables with low fat cooking spray.

2 Roast in the oven for 40 minutes until tender and beginning to char.

3 To make the sauce, place the Brie, wine and thyme leaves in a small pan set over a low heat. Stir until melted. Remove the roasting tin from the oven. Pop the roasted garlic cloves from their skins. Mash with a fork. Add to the cheese sauce.

4 Season with black pepper and serve the sauce in a dipping pot with the roasted vegetables.

Goes well with: the Rosemary and Walnut Soda Bread on **page 160**, for an extra 2 *POINTS* values per serving.

Roasted tomato and mozzarella tart

Takes 25 minutes to prepare, 15–20 minutes to cook

27 *POINTS* values per recipe

219 calories per serving

Serves 6 A lovely combination of flavours.

low fat cooking spray

450 g (1 lb) onions, sliced thinly

2 garlic cloves, sliced

2 teaspoons dried sage

1 x 213 g sheet frozen ready rolled puff pastry, defrosted

450 g (1 lb) ripe plum tomatoes, sliced thinly

1 x 125 g pack mozzarella light, drained and sliced into 6 pieces

salt and freshly ground black pepper

1 Lightly coat a lidded saucepan with low fat cooking spray and heat until hot. Add the onions and garlic and cook, stirring, for 1 minute. Add 1 tablespoon of water together with the sage. Cover with a tight fitting lid and leave on a low heat for 10 minutes, stirring occasionally, until the onions have caramelised. Remove from the heat and leave to cool slightly.

2 Preheat the oven to Gas Mark 6/200°C/fan oven 180°C. Unwrap the pastry and roll out to a thickness of 3 mm (⅛ inch). Trim the edges and score all the way round about 2 cm (¾ inch) from the edge. Place on a baking tray.

3 Spread the onions out over the pastry and arrange the tomato slices in overlapping rows on top. Top with the mozzarella slices, sprinkling over a little seasoning.

4 Bake for 15–20 minutes until the pastry is golden and the tomatoes slightly charred.

5 Divide into six portions to serve.

Serving suggestion Serve with a watercress and spinach salad, for no additional *POINTS* values.

Blue cheese and broccoli soufflés

Takes 20 minutes to prepare, 45 minutes to cook + cooling

10 *POINTS* values per recipe

140 calories per serving

Serves 4 These soufflés really work and the secret is baking them twice, so give them a go.

low fat cooking spray
110 g (4 oz) broccoli, chopped
15 g (½ oz) low fat polyunsaturated margarine
1 garlic clove, crushed
25 g (1 oz) plain flour
175 ml (6 fl oz) skimmed milk
2 eggs, separated
40 g (1½ oz) Danish blue cheese
1 egg white
salt and freshly ground black pepper

1 Preheat the oven to Gas Mark 4/180°C/fan oven 160°C. Spray 4 x 200 ml (7 fl oz) ovenproof ramekins with low fat cooking spray.

2 Bring a small pan of water to the boil and cook the broccoli for 5 minutes until tender. Drain well and mash.

3 Melt the margarine in a saucepan, add the garlic and flour and cook, stirring, for 1 minute until the mixture forms a ball. Remove from the heat and gradually add the milk, stirring until smooth after each addition. Return to the heat and cook over a low heat, stirring continuously until thickened. Season. Cool slightly before beating in the egg yolks, broccoli and cheese.

4 In a clean, grease free bowl, whisk the egg whites until stiff. Add a spoonful to the broccoli mix to slacken it and then carefully fold in the broccoli mix to the remaining whites. Spoon the mixture into the ramekins.

5 Place the ramekins in a roasting tin filled with sufficient hot water to come about a third of the way up the sides of the dishes. Bake for 20 minutes until puffed up and golden on top. Remove from the oven and allow the roasting tin to cool. They will sink at this point. When cool, loosen and then tip out, cooked side up, on to a baking tray lined with non stick baking parchment.

6 For the second baking, preheat the oven to Gas Mark 4/180°C/fan oven 160°C. Cook the soufflés for 25 minutes until puffed up again. Serve immediately.

Serving suggestion Serve with a zero *POINTS* value green salad and a handful of cherry tomatoes.

Tip Make these up to 24 hours in advance. Cook once, cool and then remove from the ramekins. Cover and refrigerate until required.

entertaining: **mains**

Creamy mushroom pork

Takes 30 minutes

13 *POINTS* values per recipe

321 calories per serving

Serves 4 Pork loin steaks are low in fat and although this sauce looks and tastes really creamy, it uses low fat soft cheese. Try adding 1 tablespoon wholegrain mustard to the sauce instead of the tarragon for the same ***POINTS*** values per serving.

low fat cooking spray

125 g (4½ oz) chestnut mushrooms, sliced

1 garlic clove, crushed

300 ml (10 fl oz) vegetable stock

100 g (3½ oz) low fat soft cheese

1 tablespoon freshly chopped tarragon

4 x 125 g (4½ oz) pork loin steaks

1 Lightly coat a saucepan with low fat cooking spray and, when sizzling, add the mushrooms. Cook over a medium heat until the mushroom juices have evaporated, about 7 minutes.

2 Add the garlic and stock and boil for 3 minutes until reduced by about a third. Whisk in the low fat soft cheese and tarragon. Remove from the heat.

3 Preheat the grill to medium and cook the pork steaks for 8–10 minutes, turning once, until golden and cooked through.

4 Warm the sauce and serve spooned over the steaks.

Serving suggestion Serve with cooked courgettes, for no additional ***POINTS*** values.

Duck à l'orange

Takes 30 minutes
5 *POINTS* values per recipe
167 calories per serving

Serves 2 Duck and orange is a classic combination and this quick recipe would make an excellent special dinner for two.

low fat cooking spray
2 x 100 g (3½ oz) skinless boneless duck breasts
1 orange
200 ml (7 fl oz) chicken stock
110 g (4 oz) carrots, peeled and cut into julienne sticks
   (see Tip)
steamed savoy cabbage, to serve

1 Lightly coat a non stick frying pan with low fat cooking spray and heat until hot. Add the duck breasts and cook for 3–4 minutes, turning until browned all over.
2 Take the zest from the orange using a zester or grater and then remove the skin with a sharp knife and segment the orange, collecting any juice. Add the orange zest, segments and any juice to the pan with the stock. Simmer for 10 minutes until the duck is just tender.
3 Add the carrots and cook for a further 5 minutes.
4 Serve with steamed cabbage.

Tip To make julienne carrots, use a vegetable peeler to cut thin ribbons along the length of the carrot and then cut these into thin narrow strips. Alternatively, cut into small, thin sticks.

Goes well with: the Parsnip Purée on **page 154**, for an extra 2 *POINTS* values per serving.

entertaining: **mains**

Chilli chicken with flageolet beans

Takes 10 minutes to prepare, 25 minutes to cook

8 *POINTS* values per recipe

351 calories per serving

Serves 2 Baking everything in one roasting tin preserves all the delicious juices.

low fat cooking spray

2 x 150 g (5½ oz) skinless boneless chicken breasts

2 garlic cloves, sliced

6 tomatoes on the vine, vine removed

1 x 410 g can flageolet beans, drained

2 tablespoons balsamic vinegar

2 teaspoons chilli flakes

1 Preheat the oven to Gas Mark 6/200°C/fan oven 180°C.

2 Lightly coat a non stick frying pan with low fat cooking spray and heat until hot. Add the chicken breasts and fry for 3–4 minutes until golden on both sides.

3 Mix together the remaining ingredients and tip into a roasting tin with 2 tablespoons water. Place the chicken breasts on top, pushing them down slightly so that they nestle in the beans.

4 Cook for 25 minutes until the chicken is tender and cooked through.

Serving suggestion Serve with a simple green salad, for no extra *POINTS* values.

Tip Try this with skinless boneless duck breast instead of chicken, for a *POINTS* value of 5 per serving.

Sesame and orange roasted carrots

Ⓥ vegan

Takes 15 minutes to prepare, 45 minutes to cook

1½ POINTS values per recipe

58 calories per serving

Serves 4 This easy side dish is delicious with roast meat; the orange perfectly accentuates the sweet carrot flavour and the sesame adds a little crunch.

350 g (12 oz) carrots, peeled and cut into thick chunks
low fat cooking spray
zest and juice 1 large orange
1 tablespoon sesame seeds
salt and freshly ground black pepper

1 Preheat the oven to Gas Mark 5/190°C/fan oven 170°C.

2 Place the carrots in a single layer in a roasting tin. Lightly coat with low fat cooking spray, season and cook for 30 minutes.

3 Remove from the oven and sprinkle over the orange zest and juice. Return to the oven for a further 15 minutes until tender and beginning to brown.

4 Sprinkle over the sesame seeds and roast for another 5 minutes until the seeds are golden.

Tip Try adding 4 garlic cloves, halved, with the orange juice for extra flavour and no additional *POINTS* values.

Sprouting broccoli with capers

Y vegan

Takes 10 minutes

0 *POINTS* values per recipe

48 calories per serving

Serves 2 Sprouting broccoli can be purple or white and is really an early spring vegetable. However, you can get tender stem broccoli, which is virtually the same, most of the year round in supermarkets.

250 g (9 oz) sprouting broccoli, tough ends trimmed

for the dressing

2 tablespoons capers, drained and chopped finely

zest and juice of ½ lemon

1 small garlic clove, crushed

1 Bring a large saucepan of water to the boil and steam the broccoli for 3–4 minutes over the water in a steaming basket until just tender (see Tip).

2 Place all the ingredients for the dressing in a small pan and warm through for 1–2 minutes.

3 Place the broccoli in a warmed serving dish and pour over the dressing.

Tips Steaming is the best way to preserve the nutrients in broccoli, but if you don't have a steamer, boil for 3–4 minutes until tender and drain well.

This dressing also works well with cooked leeks.

Twice baked herby potatoes

Y

Takes 10 minutes to prepare, 1 hour to cook

10½ *POINTS* values per recipe

155 calories per serving

Serves 4 These are great as a side dish for grilled meat or fish. On Bonfire night, serve them with 1 thick low fat sausage per person, for an additional *POINTS* value of 1½ per serving.

4 x 175 g (6 oz) baking potatoes

3 tablespoons snipped chives

2 tablespoons freshly chopped parsley

4 tablespoons low fat soft cheese

salt and freshly ground black pepper

1 Preheat the oven to Gas Mark 5/190°C/fan oven 170°C. Place the potatoes on a baking tray and cook for 45 minutes until tender.

2 Remove from the oven, halve and scoop out the soft potato inside. Mix together with the chives, parsley and soft cheese. Season.

3 Refill the potato skins and return to the oven for 15 minutes to heat through.

Tip You can prepare these potatoes ahead of time. Follow the recipe to step 3, refilling the skins, cool, cover and chill until required. Heat through in the oven for 25 minutes until hot.

Vegetable purées

These are a different way to serve vegetables. Some of the more starchy ones, such as parsnip or sweet potato, make a great low **POINTS** value substitute for potatoes. Follow the general method below for each version, stirring in any flavourings with the salt and pepper.

General method for purées
Takes 20 minutes

1 Bring a large lidded pan of water to the boil and add the vegetables. Cover and simmer for 15 minutes until tender. Drain well, then mash.
2 Cool slightly before stirring in the yogurt, milk or fromage frais, according to the recipe and then add the herbs and seasoning according to the recipe.

Parsnip

4 POINTS values per recipe
135 calories per serving
Serves 2

400 g (14 oz) parsnips, peeled and chopped
25 g (1 oz) virtually fat free fromage frais
salt and freshly ground black pepper

Tips The purée should have a slightly softer consistency than mashed potato. You can purée in the food processor if you prefer or with a hand blender.

Try adding 1–2 teaspoons of orange or lemon zest with the seasoning for extra flavour and no additional **POINTS** values.

Sweet potato and caraway

5½ *POINTS* values per recipe
185 calories per serving
Serves 2

400 g (14 oz) sweet potatoes, peeled and cut into chunks
25 g (1 oz) low fat plain yogurt
2 teaspoons caraway seeds, dry fried for 1–2 minutes until popping
salt and freshly ground black pepper

Carrot and coriander

½ *POINTS* values per recipe
45 calories per serving
Serves 2

300 g (10½ oz) carrots, peeled and cut into chunks
25 g (1 oz) 0% fat Greek yogurt
2 tablespoons freshly chopped coriander
salt and freshly ground black pepper

Brussels sprouts and parsley

½ *POINTS* values per recipe
70 calories per serving
Serves 2

300 g (10½ oz) Brussels sprouts, trimmed and halved
3 tablespoons skimmed milk
2 tablespoons freshly chopped parsley
salt and freshly ground black pepper

No Weight Watchers cookbook would be complete without some gorgeous puddings and bakes to tempt you. Take your pick from Rosemary and Walnut Soda Bread, Lemon Angel Cake, Pistachio Biscotti or Strawberry and Vanilla Cookies. Then there's also the Mocha Meringues, Orange Profiteroles with Chocolate Sauce and Rich Chocolate Mousse Cake. All of these fabulous recipes are low in **POINTS** values too.

There are plenty of puddings to choose from if you are following the **Core Plan**, from Strawberry Mousses and Blueberry Fools to Creamy Cinnamon Bananas and Spiced Carrot Puddings.

So yes, you can have your cake and eat it too.

bakes and puddings

bakes: page 158 **puddings:** page 170

Savoury mini muffins

 ❄

Takes 20 minutes
12½ POINTS values per recipe
51 calories per serving

Makes 16 These mini muffins make a great alternative to bread. Try them with soup, salad or on their own as a tasty snack.

150 g (5½ oz) self raising flour
1 teaspoon baking powder
2 teaspoons freshly chopped thyme
4 × 15 g (½ oz) sun dried tomatoes, reconstituted
    according to the packet instructions
1 egg
1 egg white
40 g (1½ oz) low fat polyunsaturated margarine,
    melted
low fat cooking spray (if needed)
salt and freshly ground black pepper

1 Preheat the oven to Gas Mark 6/200°C/fan oven 180°C. If you don't have a non stick muffin tin, lay 16 paper cases on a baking tray.
2 Sift the flour and baking powder into a large bowl. Stir in the thyme and season with a little salt and pepper. Drain the tomatoes, reserving 3 tablespoons of the soaking liquid and dry them. Cut into small pieces and stir into the flour.
3 Beat together the egg and egg white. Add the margarine and reserved soaking liquid and then add this to the flour mix quickly. Do not beat. Spray the muffin tin with low fat cooking spray and spoon the mixture into the tin or into the paper cases. Bake for 8–10 minutes until risen and golden. Serve warm or cold.

Ⓥ Tips Try adding two Quorn bacon style rashers, cooked until crisp and crumbled into the flour with the thyme, for no additional **POINTS** values.

The muffins are best if eaten the same day, but you could freeze them and warm through in the oven once defrosted. Alternatively, they can be stored in an airtight container for up to 2 days.

Caraway grissini

Ⓥ vegan

**Takes 25 minutes to prepare + 40 minutes rising,
15–20 minutes to bake**

5 *POINTS* **values per recipe**

29 calories per serving

Makes 12 These rustic breadsticks are very useful for a lunch box or a great way to enjoy dips.

low fat cooking spray

1 garlic clove, chopped finely

100 g (3½ oz) strong white bread flour (2 teaspoons reserved for rolling)

½ teaspoon salt

1 teaspoon caraway seeds

½ teaspoon easy blend yeast

sea salt flakes

1 Lightly coat a small non stick frying pan with low fat cooking spray and heat until hot. Add the garlic and cook for 2–3 minutes until beginning to brown.

2 Put the flour and salt in a bowl and stir in the garlic and caraway seeds. Blend the yeast with 75 ml (3 fl oz) warm water and pour over the flour. Mix to a soft dough, kneading lightly, then cover and leave in a warm place to double in size for 20–30 minutes.

3 Preheat the oven to Gas Mark 6/200°C/fan oven 180°C. Line a baking tray with non stick baking parchment.

4 Dust the work surface with the reserved flour and form the dough into a ball, kneading lightly. Divide into 12 equal pieces. Roll each into a thin sausage about 20 cm (8 inch) long, and place on the baking tray. Leave for 10 minutes to rise a little, then spray with low fat cooking spray, sprinkle with sea salt flakes and bake for 15–20 minutes until golden and crisp.

Tip Store the breadsticks in an airtight container for up to 4 days.

Rosemary and walnut soda bread

Ⓥ ❄

Takes 15 minutes to prepare, 20–30 minutes to bake

17 *POINTS* **values per recipe**

134 calories per serving

Serves 8 Soda bread is quick and easy to make.

225 g (8 oz) self raising flour

1 teaspoon baking powder

1 tablespoon freshly chopped rosemary

25 g (1 oz) walnuts, toasted and chopped

25 g (1 oz) low fat polyunsaturated margarine

150 ml (5 fl oz) buttermilk

salt and freshly ground black pepper

1 Preheat the oven to Gas Mark 7/220°C/fan oven 200°C. Line a baking tray with non stick baking parchment.

2 Sift the flour and baking powder into a large bowl. Stir in the rosemary and walnuts then season.

3 Add the margarine and use your fingers to rub it in. Add the buttermilk, stirring until the mixture comes together to form a soft, scone like dough. If it is too dry, add a little water.

4 Shape the dough into a circle about 18 cm (7 inch) round. Place on the baking tray and, using a sharp knife, mark into eight wedges on the top. Bake for 20–30 minutes until golden and it sounds hollow when tapped.

Tips Day old soda bread can be toasted to freshen it up.

Buttermilk is cultured skimmed milk, which is then heat treated to kill off the bacteria and stop the fermentation. If you can't find it, use 100 ml (3½ fl oz) low fat plain yogurt mixed with 50 ml (2 fl oz) skimmed milk, for the same *POINTS* values.

Vanilla and rhubarb cake

 ❄

Takes 20 minutes to prepare, 30–40 minutes to bake
+ cooling
31 *POINTS* values per recipe
250 calories per serving

Serves 8 A speedy, all in one cake that keeps moist for a couple of days and works well as a pudding with low fat custard.

400 g (14 oz) rhubarb, cut into 5 cm (2 inch) pieces
250 g (9 oz) self raising flour
1 teaspoon bicarbonate of soda
175 g (6 oz) soft dark brown sugar
75 g (2¾ oz) low fat polyunsaturated margarine, melted
2 eggs, beaten
2 teaspoons vanilla extract
2 teaspoons caster sugar, for sprinkling over

1 Place the rhubarb in a lidded pan with 2 tablespoons water. Cover and simmer for 10 minutes until pulpy. Cool slightly.
2 Preheat the oven to Gas Mark 4/180°C/fan oven 160°C. Line the base of a 20 cm (8 inch) deep cake tin with non stick baking parchment.
3 Sift the flour and bicarbonate of soda into a large bowl. Stir in the sugar, melted margarine, eggs, vanilla extract and cooled rhubarb. Mix well and pour into the prepared tin.
4 Bake for 30–40 minutes until springy and a skewer inserted in the centre comes out clean. Cool in the tin for 5 minutes before turning out to cool completely on a wire rack. Sprinkle over the caster sugar while still warm.

Tip Serve with a tablespoon of half fat crème fraîche, for a *POINTS* value of 5½ per serving.

Lemon angel cake

Takes 10 minutes to prepare, 20–30 minutes to bake
20½ *POINTS* values per recipe
142 calories per serving

Serves 10 A lusciously light and tangy lemon cake. Decorate with flowers to make a lovely centrepiece.

low fat cooking spray
4 eggs, separated
125 g (4½ oz) golden caster sugar
zest 1 lemon
½ teaspoon salt
75 g (2¾ oz) self raising flour, sifted

for the icing
80 g (3 oz) icing sugar, sifted
1½ tablespoons fresh lemon juice

1 Preheat the oven Gas Mark 5/190°C/fan oven 170°C. Lightly coat a 23 cm (9 inch) ring mould with low fat cooking spray.
2 Place the egg yolks, half the sugar, the lemon zest and salt in a bowl. Whisk until thick and pale.
3 In a separate, grease free bowl (not forgetting to clean the whisks) whisk the egg whites until they hold stiff peaks. Gradually whisk in the remaining sugar until thick and glossy.
4 Carefully fold the flour into the egg white mixture in batches, followed by the egg yolk mix. Spoon into the tin and bake for 20–30 minutes until a skewer inserted in the centre comes out clean. Cool for 10 minutes in the tin, before carefully loosening the cake with a round ended knife and inverting it on to a wire rack to cool completely.
5 To make the icing, mix together the icing sugar and lemon juice and pour over the cake so that it drips down the sides.

Tip Exchange the lemon for an orange or a lime. The *POINTS* values will remain the same.

Apple, pear and hazelnut cake

Takes 25 minutes to prepare, 1 hour 25 minutes to
bake

34 *POINTS* values per recipe

180 calories per serving

Serves 12 This is a lovely moist cake which keeps
well in an airtight container for 2–3 days. The
addition of semolina is a low fat alternative to
ground almonds and it helps to give the cake a
crumbly texture. It is delicious served either warm
or cold.

175 g (6 oz) small pears, cored and sliced

75 g (2¾ oz) red apple, cored and sliced

juice ½ lemon

125 g (4½ oz) low fat polyunsaturated margarine

150 g (5½ oz) soft light brown sugar

½ teaspoon vanilla extract

2 eggs, beaten

150 g (5½ oz) plain flour

1 teaspoon baking powder

40 g (1½ oz) semolina

75 ml (3 fl oz) skimmed milk

25 g (1 oz) hazelnuts, chopped roughly

½ teaspoon icing sugar, for dusting

1 Preheat the oven to Gas Mark 3/160°C/fan oven
140°C. Line a 20 cm (8 inch) round cake tin with
non stick baking parchment.

2 Mix the pear and apple slices with the lemon
juice to stop them going brown.

3 In a large bowl, whisk together the margarine
and sugar until pale and creamy. Add the vanilla
extract and gradually beat in the eggs.

4 Sift together the flour and baking powder and
fold them into the creamed mixture with the
semolina and milk. The mixture should have a soft
dropping consistency.

5 Spoon into the prepared tin and level the
surface. Scatter over the apple and pear slices
and the hazelnuts, drizzling with any remaining
lemon juice. Bake for 1 hour 10 minutes to 1 hour
25 minutes until a skewer inserted in the centre
comes out clean.

6 Dust with icing sugar and serve this cake warm
or cold.

Tips You can peel the fruit if you prefer but the skin
adds flavour and colour, not to mention fibre.

Pecans make an excellent alternative to hazelnuts.
The *POINTS* values will remain the same.

Orange and lemon rounds

Takes 10 minutes to prepare + 30 minutes chilling,
   10–15 minutes to bake + cooling
8 *POINTS* values per recipe
24 calories per serving

Makes 20 These delicate cookies just melt in the mouth and are great with a mid morning coffee or as an after dinner treat.

25 g (1 oz) low fat polyunsaturated margarine
25 g (1 oz) soft light brown sugar
25 g (1 oz) ground almonds
25 g (1 oz) cut mixed peel
25 g (1 oz) plain flour, sifted
zest ½ lemon
1 teaspoon orange zest

1 Preheat the oven to Gas Mark 3/160°C/fan oven 140°C. Line two baking trays with non stick baking parchment.
2 Cream together the margarine and sugar with a wooden spoon until well combined. Add the remaining ingredients and mix well. Spoon on to a piece of clingfilm and roll into a sausage. Chill for 30 minutes.
3 Slice the mixture into 20 rounds and place, well spaced out, on the baking trays. Cook for 10–15 minutes until golden. Leave to cool for 5 minutes then transfer to a wire rack to cool completely.

Tip These are best if eaten on the same day. You can keep the uncooked mixture wrapped in the fridge for up to 5 days – simply cut off what you want to bake.

Banana caramel cake

Takes 20 minutes to prepare, 45 minutes to bake + cooling
28½ *POINTS* values per recipe
236 calories per serving

Serves 8 A lovely moist banana cake.

low fat cooking spray
50 g (1¾ oz) low fat polyunsaturated margarine, melted
110 g (4 oz) soft light brown sugar
325 g (11½ oz) bananas, peeled and mashed
1 egg, beaten
zest 1 lime
175 g (6 oz) self raising flour
½ teaspoon bicarbonate of soda
1 teaspoon mixed spice

for the topping
75 g (2¾ oz) golden caster sugar
juice 1 lime

1 Preheat the oven to Gas Mark 4/180°C/fan oven 160°C. Line the base of a 20 cm (8 inch) cake tin with non stick baking parchment and lightly coat with low fat cooking spray.
2 Place the margarine, sugar, bananas, egg and lime zest in a large bowl with 2 tablespoons water and beat well.
3 Sift in the flour, bicarbonate of soda and spice. Stir until well combined. Pour into the prepared cake tin and bake for 45 minutes, until a skewer inserted into the centre comes out clean. Leave to cool in the tin for 5 minutes before inverting on to a wire rack to cool completely.
4 For the topping, place the sugar and lime juice in a small pan and heat gently until the sugar is dissolved. Simmer until golden. Remove from the heat and pour over the cake. Score eight slices through the caramel before it sets hard.

Strawberry and vanilla cookies

Takes 10 minutes to prepare, 15 minutes to bake + cooling
21 *POINTS* values per recipe
137 calories per serving

Makes 10 These delicious cookies are similar to rock cakes but hide a strawberry surprise inside.

225 g (8 oz) self raising flour
60 g (2 oz) low fat polyunsaturated margarine
60 g (2 oz) caster sugar (2 teaspoons reserved)
1 egg, beaten
4 tablespoons skimmed milk
1 teaspoon vanilla extract
25 g (1 oz) reduced sugar strawberry jam

1 Preheat the oven to Gas Mark 6/200°C/fan oven 180°C. Line a baking tray with non stick baking parchment.
2 Sift the flour into a bowl. Add the margarine and rub in using your fingers until the mixture resembles breadcrumbs. Stir in the sugar, then add the egg, milk and vanilla and mix to a soft dough.
3 Divide into 10 equal balls. Flatten each ball, spoon a little jam into the centre and shape again into a ball, sealing in the jam.
4 Place on the baking tray, sprinkle with the reserved sugar and bake for 15 minutes until golden. Transfer to a wire rack to cool.

Tip This recipe also works well with 1 teaspoon orange zest in place of the vanilla extract and reduced sugar marmalade instead of jam, for no additional **POINTS** values.

Pistachio biscotti

Takes 15 minutes to prepare, 45 minutes to bake + 15 minutes cooling
16 *POINTS* values per recipe
115 calories per serving

Makes 10 Biscotti means 'twice baked' and that's exactly what happens to these crunchy biscuits, which are great for dipping into coffee. They can be stored in an airtight container for up to a week.

110 g (4 oz) plain flour
½ teaspoon baking powder
50 g (1¾ oz) low fat polyunsaturated margarine
zest ½ orange
75 g (2¾ oz) soft light brown sugar
50 g (1¾ oz) chopped pistachios
1 teaspoon instant coffee, dissolved in 2 teaspoons hot water
1 egg white

1 Preheat the oven to Gas Mark 4/180°C/fan oven 160°C. Line a baking tray with non stick baking parchment.
2 Sift the flour and baking powder into a large bowl. Add the margarine and rub in until it resembles breadcrumbs. Stir in the orange zest, sugar and pistachios.
3 Add the dissolved coffee and egg white and knead to a soft dough, adding a little water if it is too dry.
4 Shape the dough into a log 5 cm (2 inch) wide and 5 cm (2 inch) high. Place on the baking tray and bake for 35 minutes until golden and firm.
5 Remove from the oven and cool for 15 minutes on the baking tray and then cut into 10 slices. Lay them side down on the baking tray and bake again for 10 minutes until golden.

Tip Try using chopped almonds instead of the pistachios, for a **POINTS** value of 2 per serving.

Apple and raisin charlottes

Takes 25 minutes to prepare, 25 minutes to bake
10 *POINTS* values per recipe
355 calories per serving

Serves 4 Delicious individual pudding basins.

425 g (15 oz) eating apples, peeled, cored and chopped
25 g (1 oz) soft light brown sugar
25 g (1 oz) raisins, sultanas or chopped dried dates
4 slices medium white bread, crusts removed
   (94 g total weight without crusts)
low fat cooking spray
1 tablespoon golden caster sugar
2 tablespoons maple syrup, warmed, to serve

1 Preheat the oven to Gas Mark 4/180°C/fan oven 160°C. Place the apples in a saucepan with the brown sugar, raisins or sultanas and 2 tablespoons water. Cover and simmer for 5 minutes until soft and pulpy. Remove from the heat.
2 Use a rolling pin to roll the bread thinner. Spray the insides of four 150 ml (5½ oz) pudding basins lightly with low fat cooking spray. Cut a square from one corner of a bread slice to use as a lid and then use the remainder of the bread to line a basin. Repeat with the remaining slices and basins.
3 Spoon the apple mixture into the basins to within 1 cm (½ inch) of the top. Finish with the reserved bread square to cover the apple.
4 Bake for 20 minutes. Loosen the sides with a knife and carefully invert on to a baking tray. Sprinkle over the caster sugar and bake for a further 5 minutes until golden.
5 Serve the puddings with the warmed maple syrup poured over.

Tip Try adding the zest of 1 small lemon or 1 teaspoon orange zest to the apple mixture before spooning into the moulds.

Fruits of the forest steamed pudding

Takes 25 minutes to prepare, 1 hour 20 minutes to steam
25 *POINTS* values per recipe
269 calories per serving

Serves 6 A scone crust reduces the **POINTS** values.

225 g (8 oz) self raising flour
1 teaspoon baking powder
110 g (4 oz) low fat polyunsaturated margarine
50 g (1¾ oz) golden caster sugar
150 ml (5 fl oz) skimmed milk
1 x 500 g packet frozen black fruits of the forest, defrosted

1 Sift the flour and baking powder into a bowl. Add the margarine and rub in with fingertips until the mixture resembles breadcrumbs.
2 Stir in a tablespoon of the sugar and then mix to a dough with the milk. Reserving a third, line an 850 ml (1½ pints) heatproof basin with the dough.
3 Mix 300 g (10½ oz) of the fruit with the remaining sugar. Spoon into the basin. Place the remaining dough on top, spreading to reach the sides. It will be thin, but will rise on cooking.
4 To steam, cover with a lid or folded piece of non stick baking parchment, secured with string. Bring a large pan of water to the boil, and place the pudding in a steamer on top. The water level should be below the steamer. Steam for 1 hour 20 minutes until risen and dry on the top. Check during cooking to ensure the pan doesn't boil dry.
5 Place the remaining fruit in a saucepan with 3 tablespoons water and simmer for 3–4 minutes. Remove from the heat and push through a nylon sieve to form a sauce. Discard the pips.
6 Remove the pudding from the steamer, carefully loosen the sides with a knife and invert on to a serving plate. Serve with the sauce.

bakes and puddings: **puddings**

Peach and plum crumblies

Ⓨ vegan without the yogurt ❄
Takes 15 minutes to prepare, 20–30 minutes to bake
6½ POINTS values per recipe
204 calories per serving

Serves 2 This is similar to a crumble but it's made with individual fruits, so it's easier to portion control.

2 ripe peaches or nectarines, stoned and halved
2 plums, stoned and halved
4 tablespoons orange juice
25 g (1 oz) demerara sugar
30 g (1¼ oz) plain flour
15 g (½ oz) low fat polyunsaturated margarine
2 tablespoons 0% fat Greek yogurt, to serve

1 Preheat the oven to Gas Mark 5/190°C/fan oven 170°C.
2 Divide the fruits between two ovenproof gratin dishes, cut side up, so that they sit snugly. Pour over the orange juice and sprinkle with 2 teaspoons each of the sugar.
3 Place the flour in a bowl and rub in the margarine. Stir in the remaining sugar and spoon a little on top of each piece of fruit.
4 Bake for 20–30 minutes until just soft. Serve warm with a tablespoon of Greek yogurt per serving.

Tips Ripe fruit tends to require less sugar so try to choose fruit that smells good and is not too firm.

You could also use canned fruit for this recipe. Try a 410 g can of apricots in natural juice, drained, but reserve 4 tablespoons of the juice to use in place of the orange juice, for a **POINTS** value of 3½ per serving.

Mocha meringues

Ⓨ
Takes 20 minutes to prepare, 1 hour to bake + 1 hour cooling
20 POINTS values per recipe
126 calories per serving

Makes 8 Coffee meringues look, and taste, decadent – sandwiched together with cream and chocolate.

2 egg whites
110 g (4 oz) caster sugar
2 teaspoons instant coffee, dissolved in 1 teaspoon hot water
40 g (1½ oz) dark chocolate (minimum 70% cocoa solids)
75 ml (3 fl oz) whipping cream
2 teaspoons icing sugar, sifted

1 Preheat the oven to Gas Mark 2/150°C/fan oven 130°C. Line two baking trays with non stick baking parchment.
2 In a clean bowl, whisk the egg whites until they hold stiff peaks. Add 1 tablespoon of the sugar and whisk until combined. Repeat with the remaining sugar and whisk until the meringue is stiff and glossy. Whisk in the dissolved coffee.
3 Spoon a tablespoon of the meringue on to the baking tray, flattening slightly. Repeat to make 16 rounds. Bake for 1 hour. Turn off the oven and leave to cool for a further hour in the oven.
4 To make the filling, melt the chocolate in a small saucepan over a medium heat. Whip the cream until it holds soft peaks. Stir in the chocolate and icing sugar. The cream will firm up as the chocolate sets, so when firm enough use the cream to sandwich the meringues. Serve two each.

Tip Store the unfilled meringues in an airtight container for up to 5 days.

Orange profiteroles with chocolate sauce

Takes 25 minutes to prepare, 25 minutes to bake
29 *POINTS* values per recipe
234 calories per serving

Makes 18 (Serves 6) Choux pastry is light and crisp and easy to make. Fill the profiteroles with orange flavoured sweetened ricotta cheese.

60 g (2 oz) plain flour
40 g (1½ oz) low fat polyunsaturated margarine
1 egg
1 egg white
1 x Rich Chocolate and Orange Sauce recipe (see page 200), heated

for the filling
150 g (5½ oz) ricotta cheese
2 teaspoons orange zest
1 tablespoon icing sugar, sifted

1 Preheat the oven to Gas Mark 6/200°C/fan oven 180°C. Line two baking trays with non stick baking parchment. Sift the flour on to a plate.
2 Place the margarine in a large pan with 125 ml (4 fl oz) water. Bring to the boil then remove from the heat. Add the flour and beat thoroughly until the mixture is smooth and forms a ball.
3 Whisk together the egg and egg white and then gradually beat the egg into the flour mixture. Make sure the mixture is beaten well to incorporate the air which make the buns rise.
4 Use a teaspoon to place 18 dollops of the mixture on to the baking trays, leaving room for them to expand.
5 Bake for 20 minutes until golden. Do not open the oven otherwise the profiteroles will sink. Remove from the oven and pierce each one with a skewer to let out the steam. Return to the oven for a further 5 minutes to dry out the insides. Transfer to a wire rack to cool completely.

6 To fill, mix the filling ingredients together, then carefully slit the buns and spoon or pipe in the mixture. Serve three each, with the hot Rich Chocolate and Orange Sauce.

Tip Do not fill the buns more than 2 hours before serving otherwise they will go soggy. Try to make the buns fresh that day.

Goes well with: the Cheat's Toffee Sauce on **page 201** instead of the Rich Chocolate and Orange Sauce, for 4½ *POINTS* values per serving.

bakes and puddings: **puddings**

Chocolate and raspberry pots

Takes 15 minutes + 30 minutes chilling
15½ *POINTS* values per recipe
208 calories per serving

Serves 4 These rich puds deliver that fantastic hit of chocolate, with just a hint of raspberry. They're also ideal for entertaining since you can make them up to 4 hours in advance.

150 g (5½ oz) raspberries, defrosted if frozen
100 g (3½ oz) dark chocolate (minimum 70% cocoa solids), broken into pieces
1 egg, separated
1 egg white
2 tablespoons caster sugar

1 Reserve eight raspberries for decoration. Then push the remaining raspberries through a nylon sieve to make a purée. Discard the pips.
2 Melt the chocolate in a heatproof bowl set over a pan of simmering water. Remove from the heat, cool slightly and then beat in the egg yolk and raspberry purée.
3 In a clean, grease free bowl, whisk the egg whites until they hold stiff peaks. Whisk in the sugar until glossy.
4 Carefully fold the chocolate raspberry mixture into the egg whites and mix well. Spoon into serving glasses and chill for at least 30 minutes until set. Decorate with the reserved raspberries before serving.

Tips Try strawberries instead of the raspberries – you might need to blitz the fruit in a food processor to get a purée. The *POINTS* values will remain the same.

1 teaspoon orange zest also works well in addition to the raspberry or strawberry purée.

Strawberry tiramisu

Takes 20 minutes + 20 minutes – 1 hour chilling
5½ *POINTS* values per recipe
187 calories per serving

Serves 2 Serve these pretty layered desserts in elegant tall glasses for extra effect.

8 sponge fingers (40 g/1½ oz in total)
4 tablespoons orange juice
150 g (5½ oz) strawberries
125 g (4½ oz) fat free plain fromage frais
1½ tablespoons caster sugar

1 Break the sponge fingers into pieces and place half of them in the bottom of two glasses. Drizzle over a little of the orange juice.
2 Hull and chop the strawberries, reserving two for decoration. Place a spoonful on top of the sponge fingers in each glass.
3 Mix together the fromage frais and sugar. Spoon half the mixture on top of the strawberries, dividing it between the two glasses.
4 Add the remaining half of the sponge fingers, followed by the remaining strawberries and the fromage frais mixture to each of the two glasses.
5 Decorate with a whole strawberry and then chill for 20 minutes to an hour before serving.

Tip If you prefer, use 125 g (4½ oz) flavoured yogurt – raspberry, strawberry or orange would work well – instead of the fromage frais and sugar, for a *POINTS* value of 2½ per serving.

Apricot and pecan filo tart

Takes 20 minutes to prepare, 10–15 minutes to bake
18½ *POINTS* values per recipe
195 calories per serving

Serves 6 This is a low fat version of a French fruit tart which uses filo pastry instead of flaky pastry. It's best eaten the same day, warm from the oven.

low fat cooking spray
6 x 14 g sheets filo pastry
1 x 410 g can apricots in natural juice
2 bananas, sliced into rounds
30 g (1¼ oz) pecans, chopped roughly
1 teaspoon icing sugar, to dust
6 scoops low fat ice cream, to serve

1 Preheat the oven to Gas Mark 6/200°C/fan oven 180°C. Lightly coat a 30 x 20 cm (12 x 8 inch) Swiss roll tin with low fat cooking spray.
2 Spray each filo sheet with low fat cooking spray as you go. Line the tin with the filo sheets so that they overlap each other and come just up the sides of the tin. Drain the apricots and reserve the juice. Arrange the apricots, cut side down, in rows on top of the pastry. Arrange the banana slices between the apricots.
3 Heat the reserved apricot juice in a pan and simmer for 3–5 minutes until syrupy and reduced by half, then brush over the apricots. Sprinkle over the nuts and bake for 10–15 minutes until golden.
4 Serve warm, dusted with icing sugar and accompanied by a scoop of low fat ice cream per serving.

Tip Try changing the apricots to canned peaches or varying the nuts to hazelnuts, for the same *POINTS* values per serving.

Baked poppy seed and lemon cheesecake

Takes 20 minutes to prepare, 30–40 minutes to bake + 1 hour chilling
44 *POINTS* values per recipe
290 calories per serving

Serves 8 This recipe is based on the classic New York style baked cheesecake. It keeps well in the fridge for 2–3 days.

125 g (4½ oz) reduced fat digestive biscuits, crushed
25 g (1 oz) low fat polyunsaturated margarine, melted
150 g (5½ oz) golden caster sugar
1 tablespoon cornflour, sifted
zest 2 lemons
2 teaspoons vanilla extract
300 g (10½ oz) low fat soft cheese
200 g tub 4% fat crème fraîche
110 g (4 oz) 0% fat Greek yogurt
2 eggs, beaten
1 tablespoon poppy seeds

1 Preheat the oven to Gas Mark 6/200°C/fan oven 180°C. Line the base of a 20 cm (8 inch) springform cake tin with non stick baking parchment.
2 Combine the crushed biscuits with the melted margarine and 1 tablespoon of water. Press evenly into the base of the tin. Chill until required.
3 Place the sugar, cornflour and lemon zest in a food processor and blend briefly. Add the vanilla, soft cheese, crème fraîche, yogurt and eggs and blend until smooth.
4 Pour the mixture over the base and sprinkle with the poppy seeds. Bake for 30–40 minutes until the cheesecake has begun to shrink from the sides of the tin and is golden on top – it should still wobble slightly in the middle, but will firm up on cooling. Leave to cool before removing from the tin, then chill for at least 1 hour. Don't worry if the cheesecake cracks.

Rich chocolate mousse cake

Takes 20 minutes to prepare, 40–45 minutes to bake
+ cooling

45½ *POINTS* values per recipe

199 calories per serving

Serves 12 This is a really rich, mousse like dessert cake. Made with whisked egg whites, the result is a delicious, moist and intensely chocolatey gateau. Serve warm, dusted with mixed spice and icing sugar.

125 g (4½ oz) low fat polyunsaturated margarine

250 g (9 oz) dark chocolate (minimum 70% cocoa solids), broken into pieces

3 eggs, separated

50 g (1¾ oz) golden caster sugar

1½ teaspoons mixed spice

3 egg whites

½ teaspoon icing sugar

1 Preheat the oven to Gas Mark 4/180°C/fan oven 160°C. Line the base of a 20 cm (8 inch) springform cake tin with non stick baking parchment.

2 Melt the margarine in a saucepan. Remove from the heat and add the chocolate, stirring to dissolve. If there are any lumps of chocolate left after a minute or so, return to a low heat, continue stirring until dissolved and then remove again from the heat.

3 In a large bowl, whisk the egg yolks with half the sugar and 1 teaspoon of the mixed spice until pale and thick. Fold in the chocolate mixture.

4 In a separate, clean, grease free bowl, whisk the egg whites until they form stiff peaks. Gradually whisk in the remaining sugar until the egg whites are glossy and stiff.

5 Add a large spoonful of the whites to the chocolate mixture and fold in quickly to slacken it. Carefully fold in the remaining whites until fully incorporated. Spoon into the prepared tin and bake for 40–45 minutes until risen. Cool in the tin with a piece of foil over the top to soften the crust.

6 To serve, loosen the edges with a round ended knife and remove the springform tin. Carefully slide the cake from the base and lining on to a plate. Mix together the remaining mixed spice and icing sugar and dust over the cake. Serve warm in wedges.

Tips Don't worry if the cake sinks – it's similar to a soufflé so expect it to.

It's best to enjoy it on the same day you bake it, but it can be refreshed quickly in the microwave the following day.

Strawberry mousses

Takes 10 minutes + 1 hour chilling
3 *POINTS* values per recipe
56 calories per serving

Serves 4 These fluffy mousses are great for children and adults alike.

150 g (5½ oz) ripe strawberries, hulled and chopped
100 g (3½ oz) low fat soft cheese
1 sachet strawberry sugar free jelly
150 ml (5 fl oz) boiling water
2 egg whites

1 Reserve 2 tablespoons of the strawberries and mix together the remaining strawberries with the low fat soft cheese.
2 Dissolve the jelly in the boiling water. Top up to 450 ml (16 fl oz) with cold water and then stir into the strawberry mixture. Leave to cool and refrigerate until just beginning to set.
3 In a clean bowl, whisk the egg whites until they hold stiff peaks. Carefully fold the egg whites into the jelly mixture and spoon into individual tall glasses. It will begin to set immediately.
4 Chill for about 1 hour until set and serve decorated with the reserved strawberries.

Tip Try mixing the flavours of the mousses. For example, an orange or raspberry jelly would work well with the strawberries.

Baked apples with apricot jam

 vegan

Takes 10 minutes to prepare, 25–30 minutes to bake
+ 10 minutes soaking
7½ *POINTS* values per recipe
126 calories per serving

Serves 4 These tasty apples are filled with couscous and apricots, baked in the oven and then served with apricot jam on the side.

60 g (2 oz) couscous
1 x 411 g can apricots in natural juice, drained, juice reserved
4 eating apples
4 teaspoons artificial sweetener
finely grated zest 1 lemon

1   Place the couscous in a bowl and pour over all but 2 tablespoons of the reserved juice from the apricots. Set aside to soak for 10 minutes. Meanwhile, preheat the oven to Gas Mark 4/180°C/ fan oven 160°C.
2   Core the apples down the centre, keeping them whole. Run a knife around the circumference, cutting a slit just into the skin.
3   Roughly chop six apricots. Fluff the couscous and stir in the chopped apricots, 2 teaspoons sweetener and the lemon zest. Use to fill the apples. Place in a baking tin. Mix the remaining juice with 3 tablespoons water and drizzle over the apples. Bake for 25–30 minutes until tender.
4   Blitz the remaining apricots in a food processor with the remaining 2 teaspoons sweetener to form a rough jam and serve with the apples.

Blueberry fools

Takes 5 minutes + 1 hour 10 minutes chilling
2 *POINTS* values per recipe
61 calories per serving

Serves 2 Blueberries are deliciously sweet and very good for you. Blitz them with yogurt and fromage frais for a quick and nutritious fruit fool.

150 g (5½ oz) blueberries
50 g (1¾ oz) 0% fat Greek yogurt
75 g (2¾ oz) fat free fromage frais
2 teaspoons artificial sweetener

1   Reserving 8–10 for decoration, place the blueberries in the microwave for 1 minute, then cool to room temperature for 1 hour.
2   Place the cooled blueberries in a food processor or liquidiser and whizz until roughly blended.
3   Mix together the yogurt, fromage frais and sweetener. Spoon the blueberries into a bowl and stir through the yogurt mixture creating a swirly effect. Chill for 10 minutes before serving in glass bowls decorated with the reserved blueberries.

Roasted autumn fruit salad

Takes 15 minutes to prepare, 40–50 minutes to bake
5 *POINTS* values per recipe
94 calories per serving

Serves 4 Serve this salad warm with a dollop of spiced 0% fat Greek yogurt. The cooked fruit can be kept in the fridge for up to 2 days, and served either cold or warm (heat in the microwave for 30–60 seconds).

250 g (9 oz) pears, cored and sliced

250 g (9 oz) eating apples, cored and sliced

200 g (7 oz) plums, stoned and halved

1 cinnamon stick

low fat cooking spray

2–3 tablespoons artificial sweetener, to taste, plus 1 teaspoon to serve

½ teaspoon ground cinnamon

4 tablespoons 0% fat Greek yogurt

1 Preheat the oven to Gas Mark 5/190°C/fan oven 170°C.

2 Place the fruit and the cinnamon stick in a large roasting tin and add 4 tablespoons of water. Spray generously with low fat cooking spray and bake for 40–50 minutes until the fruit is tender and beginning to char.

3 Remove the fruit from the oven, take out the cinnamon stick and sprinkle with 2 tablespoons of the sweetener, stirring to mix in. Taste to see if more sweetener is required. Don't worry if some of the plums are very soft as they will help to form a sauce.

4 To serve, mix the extra teaspoon of sweetener and ground cinnamon into the yogurt. Serve dolloped on top of the warm fruit.

Tip Bananas add a touch of natural sweetness to this salad, but don't need so long to cook – add 2 small bananas, peeled and sliced, for the final 15 minutes of cooking time, for a *POINTS* value of 2 per serving. If adding bananas, you will not be able to store the fruit as the bananas will turn black, and although still edible, don't look very nice.

Griddled tropical fruit salad

Y vegan
Takes 15 minutes
5 *POINTS* values per recipe
193 calories per serving

Serves 2 Fruit naturally caramelises on the griddle, making it sweeter and more delicious.

4 x 60 g (2 oz) slices fresh or canned pineapple
1 banana, sliced in chunks
1 small firm papaya, peeled and deseeded
low fat cooking spray

for the coulis
1 small mango, peeled and cut from the stone
zest and juice ½ lime
2 teaspoons artificial sweetener (optional)

1 To make the coulis, place the mango flesh in a food processor or liquidiser and blend until smooth. Add the lime zest and juice and blitz to mix. Taste and add the sweetener if required.
2 Heat a griddle or non stick frying pan until hot. Spray the fruit with low fat cooking spray, place in the pan and cook for 1–2 minutes, turning once, until beginning to soften and char. You may have to do this in batches.
3 Serve the fruit on plates with the coulis drizzled over.

Goes well with: a half quantity of Minted Summer Fruits Coulis on **page 202** instead of the Mango Coulis. The *POINTS* values will remain the same.

Mint and raspberry jellies

Takes 15 minutes + 1 hour chilling
½ *POINTS* value per recipe
17 calories per serving

Serves 4 These make a lovely, refreshing summer pudding and are particularly good for alfresco dining.

10 mint leaves, torn
300 ml (10 fl oz) boiling water
1 sachet raspberry sugar free jelly
125 g (4½ oz) raspberries, defrosted if frozen

1 Place the mint leaves in a jug and pour over the boiling water. Leave to infuse for 5 minutes.
2 Add the jelly to the jug and stir to dissolve. If it doesn't dissolve fully, microwave for a few seconds and stir again.
3 Reserve four raspberries and roughly crush the rest with a fork. Stir the crushed raspberries into the jelly and top up with cold water to make 600 ml (1 pint). Divide between four glasses. Cool and chill in the fridge for 1 hour until set.
4 Serve decorated with the reserved raspberries.

Tip Try this recipe using orange sugar free jelly and fresh blueberries. The *POINTS* values will remain the same.

Baked cardamom and orange custards

Takes 10 minutes to prepare, 40 minutes to bake + chilling

4½ *POINTS* values per recipe

98 calories per serving

Serves 4 These easy custards make a superb dinner party dessert.

low fat cooking spray
200 ml (7 fl oz) skimmed milk
4 cardamom pods
2 eggs, beaten
2 tablespoons artificial sweetener
2 oranges

1 Preheat the oven to Gas Mark 3/160°C/fan oven 140°C. Lightly coat four 150 ml (5 fl oz) ovenproof ramekins with low fat cooking spray.
2 Place the milk in a pan, add the seeds from the cardamom pods and gently warm until hand hot. Remove from the heat and whisk in the eggs and sweetener. Pour the mixture into the prepared ramekins, straining it through a sieve to remove any unmixed egg and the cardamom seeds.
3 Finely grate the zest from 1 orange and stir a little into each ramekin.
4 Place the ramekins in a deep roasting tin and fill with sufficient hot water to come halfway up the sides of the pots. Bake for 40 minutes until just set (they will still wobble slightly). Remove from the oven, allow to cool and then chill.
5 Use a serrated knife to slice the skin from the oranges. Segment the oranges, collecting any juice.
6 To serve, top the custards with the orange segments and juice.

Tip If you prefer, you can serve these custards warm.

Creamy cinnamon bananas

Takes 10 minutes

8½ *POINTS* values per recipe

268 calories per serving

Serves 2 Warm and creamy custard poured over bananas and dusted with cinnamon – delicious.

1 x Basic Custard recipe (see page 202)

½ teaspoon cinnamon, plus extra to dust

2 tablespoons low fat fromage frais

2 bananas

1 Prepare the custard following the recipe on page 202. Remove from the heat and whisk in the cinnamon. Cool slightly before whisking in the fromage frais.

2 Peel and slice the bananas into two serving dishes. Pour over the custard, dust with extra cinnamon and serve.

Tips To serve this cold, cool completely, cover and chill until required. It can be made up to 4 hours in advance.

Mixed spice or freshly grated nutmeg can be used as an alternative to cinnamon.

Spiced carrot puddings

Takes 10 minutes to prepare, 20 minutes to bake + 5 minutes cooling

5½ *POINTS* values per recipe

108 calories per serving

Serves 4 These individual puds are a little like passion cake with a spiced carrot mixture.

low fat cooking spray

1 small orange

110 g (4 oz) carrots, grated finely

2 eggs, beaten

1 x 250 g tub Quark

1 teaspoon mixed spice

4 teaspoons artificial sweetener

1 Preheat the oven to Gas Mark 4/180°C/fan oven 160°C. Lightly coat four ovenproof ramekins or pudding basins with low fat cooking spray.

2 Finely grate the zest from the orange, then slice the orange thinly. Place an orange slice on the base of each ramekin or pudding basin. Mix the remaining ingredients with the orange zest and spoon into the ramekins over the orange slices.

3 Place the ramekins in a small roasting tin and then fill the roasting tin with sufficient hot water to come two thirds of the way up the sides of the pots. Bake in the oven for 20 minutes until set. They should only just be turning brown on top.

4 Remove from the roasting tin and leave to cool for 5 minutes in the ramekins before loosening the sides with a knife and turning out to serve.

In this chapter you'll find recipes for sauces and dips, both sweet and savoury as well as marinades for meat, fish and tofu. They go well with many of the recipes throughout *Cook!* or you can think of your own combinations. The Balsamic, Honey and Lemon Marinade works well with grilled chicken or fresh tuna. The Tomato Pesto is fantastic stirred through hot pasta and the Thai Style Marinade works well with tofu. The Hot Chocolate and Orange Sauce turns low fat ice cream into a fantastic dessert or you can stir a spoonful of the Cheat's Toffee Sauce into 0% fat Greek yogurt for a delicious instant dessert.

sauces and
marinades

Tomato pesto

Takes 10 minutes
7½ POINTS values per recipe
98 calories per serving

Serves 4 Sun dried tomatoes make this colourful and help to keep the **POINTS** values low. Cover and store in the fridge for up to 5 days.

2 tablespoons pine nuts
4 sun dried tomatoes (15 g /½ oz total weight),
  reconstituted according to the packet instructions
15 g (½ oz) basil leaves, torn
1 tablespoon extra virgin olive oil
1 tablespoon finely grated Parmesan cheese

1 Heat a small non stick frying pan until hot and dry fry the pine nuts for 1–2 minutes until golden all over. Watch them carefully as they burn easily.
2 Drain the sun dried tomatoes, reserving the soaking liquid and chop roughly.
3 Place all the ingredients in a food processor and blend until a rough paste is formed. Add 2 tablespoons of the soaking liquid and blend again.

Balsamic, honey and lemon marinade

Ⓥ **vegan**
Takes 5 minutes + 20 minutes marinating
1 POINTS values per recipe
37 calories per serving

Serves 2 This works well on chicken or beef, but also with meaty fish such as tuna or swordfish.

3 tablespoons balsamic vinegar
2 teaspoons runny honey
zest and juice 1 lemon

1 Mix all the ingredients together and pour over the meat or fish (see Tip).
2 Cover and leave to marinate in a non metallic dish for at least 20 minutes at room temperature.

Tips Food takes longer to absorb flavours whilst being chilled. So if you are leaving something for more than 30 minutes, refrigerate and then leave to marinate for at least an hour.

Makes enough for 2 tuna or swordfish steaks, 2 chicken breasts or 2 beef steaks for weights between 100 g (3½ oz) and 150 g (5½ oz) or 150 g (5½ oz) tofu.

2 POINTS values per serving

Ginger and sesame marinade

vegan
Takes 5 minutes
1½ POINTS values per recipe
61 calories per serving

Serves 2 This works particularly well with raw prawns or chicken.

4 cm (1¾ inch) piece fresh root ginger, peeled and grated
3 tablespoons light soy sauce
1 garlic clove, crushed
2 teaspoons sesame oil

1 Combine all the ingredients and pour over the food to be marinated.
2 Mix well, cover and leave for at least 20 minutes at room temperature. (See Tip for Balsamic, Honey and Lemon Marinade on page 196).

Tips If you cut up the meat or fish, the surface area is greater so more of the flavours will be absorbed.

Makes enough for 2 chicken breasts or up to 300 g (10½ oz) prawns.

Salsa verde

vegan
Takes 10 minutes
0 POINTS values per recipe
6 calories per serving

Serves 6 This is delicious tossed into cooked pasta. Cover and store for up to 5 days in the fridge.

15 g (½ oz) each basil, parsley and mint, chopped roughly
1 teaspoon lemon zest
1 garlic clove, crushed
1 tablespoon capers in brine, drained
1 teaspoon Dijon mustard
1 tablespoon fresh lemon juice
salt and freshly ground black pepper

1 Place all the ingredients except the lemon juice in a food processor and blend briefly – it should be quite coarse still.
2 Add the lemon juice and again blend briefly to combine. Season before serving.

Tip This is ideal with grilled or barbecued meat and fish.

0 POINTS values per serving

Fresh tomato salsa

Y vegan

Takes 10 minutes

0 *POINTS* values per recipe

31 calories per serving

Serves 2 Fresh salsas are a great way to add flavour and zest to your food. Many have a zero *POINTS* value and provide extra vitamins and minerals. Try them with burgers or grilled meat. You can also use them to help fill pittas.

2 ripe tomatoes on the vine, deseeded and diced

4 cm (1¾ inch) piece cucumber, diced

½ red onion, sliced very thinly

1 tablespoon chopped coriander

1 teaspoon lime zest

1 tablespoon lime juice

1 Combine all the ingredients and mix well.

2 Chill for 5 minutes before serving.

Tip If making this ahead, combine all the ingredients except the coriander, which will discolour. Cover and chill, then add the coriander at the last minute.

0 *POINTS* values per serving

Guacamole

Y vegan

Takes 10 minutes

11 *POINTS* values per recipe

70 calories per serving

Serves 6 This Mexican dip is delicious with a selection of zero *POINTS* value crudités for dipping.

2 small avocadoes (300 g/10½ oz) peeled, stoned and flesh diced

1 red chilli, deseeded and diced finely

2 spring onions, chopped

2 tablespoons freshly chopped coriander

2 tomatoes, deseeded and diced

juice 1 lime

salt and freshly ground black pepper

1 Place the diced avocado in a large bowl and mash roughly using a fork.

2 Add all other ingredients and mix well. Season before serving.

Tip You can cover and chill this for up to 2 hours. Place the avocado stone in the bowl to prevent the avocadoes from going brown. The lime juice will also help.

2 *POINTS* values per serving

sauces: **savoury**

Thai style marinade

Takes 10 minutes
0 *POINTS* values per recipe
27 calories per serving

Serves 2 The combination of lemon grass, lime and ginger creates a fantastically fresh and authentic Thai flavour. It's especially good with fish and seafood, but also delicious with chicken and tofu.

1 lemon grass stick, tough outer stalks removed, chopped
1 small red chilli, deseeded and diced finely (optional)
1 lime leaf, shredded (see Tip)
2 cm (¾ inch) piece fresh root ginger, peeled and grated
2 teaspoons fish sauce
½ teaspoon lime zest
juice 2 limes

1 Combine all the ingredients with 1 tablespoon water and pour over the food to be marinated.
2 Mix well, cover and leave to marinate for at least 20 minutes at room temperature. (See Tip for Balsamic, Honey and Lemon Marinade on page 196).

Tips Lime leaf adds a special flavour to this combination. It is slightly sweeter than the lime itself. It can be found fresh in supermarkets, often as a combination of Thai flavoured herbs, or dried. If you manage to get a bunch of them, as is possible in an Oriental supermarket, they freeze very well.

Makes enough for 2 chicken breasts and up to 150 g (5½ oz) tofu.

Tangy chilli relish

Y vegan
Takes 10 minutes to prepare, 15 minutes to cook
0 *POINTS* values per recipe
26 calories per serving

Serves 4 As they cook, the chillies become milder.

low fat cooking spray
1 red onion, diced finely
1 garlic clove, chopped
110 g (4 oz) red chillies, deseeded and diced
2 tablespoons balsamic vinegar
2 teaspoons artificial sweetener
salt and freshly ground black pepper

1 Lightly coat a small saucepan with low fat cooking spray. Add the onion and garlic. Cook 2–3 minutes. Add the chillies, reduce the heat. Cook for 10 minutes, stirring occasionally, until tender.
2 Stir in the vinegar and sweetener. Season to taste. Cool and store in an airtight container in the fridge for up to 5 days.

Tip Try with 110 g (4 oz) grilled mackerel fillets and ribbons of cucumber, salted for 10 minutes before rinsing, for a *POINTS* value of 4½ per serving.

0 *POINTS* values per serving

Rich chocolate
and orange sauce

Takes 10 minutes
13½ *POINTS* values per recipe
175 calories per serving

Serves 4 Try this fabulous treat over ice cream or
with cake or with the profiteroles on page 174.

**100 g (3½ oz) dark chocolate (minimum 70% cocoa
    solids)**
200 ml (7 fl oz) skimmed milk
1 tablespoon golden syrup
zest 1 orange

1 Break the chocolate into pieces and then chop
into smaller pieces.
2 Warm the milk in a small pan to just below
boiling, then remove from the heat.
3 Add the chocolate to the pan and stir to dissolve.
If it doesn't quite dissolve, reheat very gently.
4 Stir in the golden syrup and orange zest.

Tips For a mocha sauce, dissolve the chocolate in
100 ml (3½ fl oz) strong black coffee, then stir in
100 ml (3½ fl oz) skimmed milk, for a ***POINTS*** value
of 3½ per serving.

Make ahead of time and chill until required. It will
set so gently reheat in a pan or in the microwave.

3½ *POINTS* values per serving

Cheat's toffee sauce

Takes 10 minutes
12 *POINTS* values per recipe
131 calories per serving

Serves 4 This is a great sauce for ice cream, meringues or simply poured over sliced bananas.

110 g (4 oz) hard toffees
50 ml (2 fl oz) skimmed milk

1 Place the toffees and milk in a small saucepan and heat very gently, stirring continuously until dissolved. This will take at least 5 minutes. Serve warm or cold.

Tip This can be made in advance, covered and refrigerated until required. Reheat gently in a pan or microwave just before serving.

Goes well with: the Mocha Meringues on **page 172**, for 4 *POINTS* values per serving.

3 *POINTS* values per serving

Tropical fruit sauce

vegan

Takes 10 minutes
2 *POINTS* values per recipe
32 calories per serving

Serves 4 Serve this over sponge cake, or to jazz up a fruit salad or simply pour over a scoop of low fat ice cream.

1 medium ripe mango
2 passionfruit
1 tablespoon lime juice
2 teaspoons artificial sweetener

1 Slice down the side of the mango, cutting the flesh off the stone, then peel and dice.
2 Halve the passionfruit and scoop out the seeds.
3 Place the mango chunks, passionfruit pulp, lime juice and sweetener in a liquidiser and blend until smooth. Add the passionfruit seeds to the sauce.

Tips Try a tropical melba sauce: substitute 75 g (2¾ oz) raspberries pushed through a sieve for the passionfruit pulp. The *POINTS* values will remain the same.

You can freeze this sauce – it works well in an ice cube tray as you can then defrost exactly the amount you need.

Minted summer fruits coulis

Ⓥ vegan ❄

Takes 10 minutes
1 *POINTS* value per recipe
23 calories per serving

Serves 4 Delicious with sponge cakes, drizzled over strawberries or as a dip for sponge fingers.

150 g (5½ oz) raspberries
150 g (5½ oz) strawberries, hulled and chopped
  roughly
4 mint leaves
1 teaspoon lemon juice
1 tablespoon artificial sweetener

1 Place the raspberries in a food processor or liquidizer. Hull and roughly chop the strawberries. Shred the mint leaves. Add to the food processor with the strawberries. Whiz until smooth.
2 Add the lemon juice and sweetener in the food processor and whiz until combined. You may need to add a little water to get a sauce consistency.

Tip Choosing ripe, naturally sweet fruit reduces the amount of sweetener required.

Basic custard

Ⓥ

Takes 10 minutes
3½ *POINTS* values per recipe
72 calories per serving

Serves 4 Use this with desserts or toss in some chopped fruit and flavour it with one of the ideas below for a different pudding. It also makes a good base for a fruit fool mixed with 0% fat Greek yogurt or fat free fromage frais.

300 ml (10 fl oz) skimmed milk
2 eggs, beaten
1 tablespoon artificial sweetener

1 Place all but 2 tablespoons of the milk in a small saucepan and heat gently.
2 Beat together the eggs and sweetener and then stir in the reserved milk.
3 Pour the warm milk over the egg mixture and mix well. Strain this mixture back into the pan to remove any egg strands.
4 Heat very gently, stirring continuously, for 2–3 minutes until the custard thinly coats the back of the spoon.

Tips Do not boil, otherwise the custard will separate.

For a vanilla flavour, add 1 teaspoon vanilla extract after straining, or add a teaspoon of ground ginger for a ginger flavour, for no additional ***POINTS*** values.

½ *POINTS* values per serving

sauces: **sweet**

Index for the Core Plan weekly *POINTS* allowance

If you're following the **Core Plan**, you have the flexibility to add non **Core** foods to your meals by using your optional Weekly *POINTS* allowance of 21.

You'll have noticed that the *POINTS* Plan recipes contain some **Core Plan** foods as ingredients. For example, in the Asparagus and Basil Tart on page 110 only the filo pastry and pine nuts are not on the **Core** Food List. So if you wanted to make this recipe as part of a **Core Plan** meal, you would need to allocate 2 *POINTS* values from your weekly allowance per serving.

With the help of this index, you can easily use the *POINTS* Plan recipes in *Cook!* as part of your 3 **Core Plan** meals a day. Below you'll find the *POINTS* Plan recipes listed alphabetically, together with the number of *POINTS* values per serving you would need to use from your weekly allowance.

If you use these recipes outside of your 3 meals a day, however, you would need to allocate the *POINTS* values shown on the original recipe, to comply with the **Core Plan** guidelines.

index